A Parent's Guide to
Teaching Art

Donna B. Gray

BETTERWAY PUBLICATIONS, INC.
WHITE HALL, VIRGINIA

Published by Betterway Publications, Inc.
P.O. Box 219
Crozet, VA 22932
(804) 823-5661

Cover design and photographs by Susan Riley
Photographs by William Swern
Typography by Park Lane Associates

Library of Congress Cataloging-in-Publication Data
Gray, Donna B.
  A parent's guide to teaching art : how to encourage your child's artistic talent and ability / Donna B. Gray.
      p. cm.
  Includes bibliographical references and index.
  ISBN 1-55870-202-4 (pbk.) : $11.95
  1. Children as artists. 2. Youth as artists. 3. Gifted children-
  -Education--Art. I. Title.
  N351.G73 1991
  700-dc20   91-4064
                                                               CIP

Printed in the United States of America
0 9 8 7 6 5 4 3 2 1

This book is dedicated in loving memory of my mother,
Dorothy Briggs,
who encouraged and supported me
in the fields of education and art.

ACKNOWLEDGMENTS

I would like to personally thank my husband, Russ, for "putting up with me" while writing this book. I would also like to thank the following: William Swern, photographer; the Indianapolis Public Library, Indianapolis, Indiana; Rockville Library, Rockville, Indiana; Greencastle Public Library, Greencastle, Indiana; DePauw University Library, Greencastle, Indiana; Terre Haute Public Library, Terre Haute, Indiana; and Crawfordsville Public Library, Crawfordsville, Indiana.

Thanks to the students of Rockville High School and their teacher, Mrs. Rita Jacks, for allowing us to come into their classroom and take photographs. Thanks to the Reverend and Mrs. Rosalie Hoover for allowing us to come into their home and take photographs. A special thanks to Mrs. Kathy Mathis and her children Kevin, Angela, and Aaron, Sarah Quackenbush, Lee Wildermuth, Renice Gray, Rita Jacks, Pamela York, and Scott Edwards for looking so nice in the photographs. Thank you to my budding artists who contributed their artwork for this book: Amy Rightsell, Erin Brewer, Carrie Williams, Scott Edwards, Jason Nye, Robert Plante, Pamela York, Cary Cosby, Colleen Cosby, Kyndel Budz, Marian Schlotterbeck, Gabrielle Fornari, Lucretia Williams, Ellen Lunsford, Chad Williams, Casandra Apathy, Linda O'Brien, Kassie Apathy, Piper Wainman, and Senah Selby.

A thank you to my son, Mark Wildermuth, who is in the Navy; your encouragement and cheers kept me working on this book. Thank you must also go to Robert Hostage, my publisher, for giving me the opportunity to write this book.

CONTENTS

INTRODUCTION

A child who is talented in the visual arts is different from other children. Quite often he will turn off the television, tell his friends he's too busy to play, and spend hours alone working on a project. He is always drawing, is very excited over new art materials, and is forever noticing the endless beauty of our world. This love for art is both exciting and a little intimidating for parents. But it doesn't have to be that way. This book is written to help you understand your child's interest in art and to give you specific things to do that will develop his or her talent.

Please do not think art is so difficult that you cannot possibly help your child. Many parents feel that way. You will not be asked to understand art yourself; you will merely be providing the information and encouragement for your child to do it himself. It would be very frustrating, time-consuming, and totally unnecessary for you to educate yourself enough to instruct your child in art. You will be told how to encourage him, how to recognize talent, and how to set up an art studio. In addition, you will be shown the pros and cons of art lessons, the careers available to artists, projects and supplies for each age group, and a list of good books and magazines. There is even a special chapter just for grandparents.

I wrote this book because I love children and understand their need for supportive and encouraging parents. I also wrote it because I love parents, too, especially the ones who want to help their children develop their talents to their full potential. Teaching art and being a parent myself has made me realize the difficulty of this task for someone who knows very little about art. It is my hope that this book will provide you with enough information to develop and encourage the artistic talent in your child.

Why study art? Even I have asked myself that question every so often. The visual arts satisfy your child's personal need for display, celebration, expression, and communication. Everyday objects are transformed from purely functional objects to things of beauty; blank walls become areas of communication. The visual arts include all objects that are appealing to the eye, including photography, film making, sculpture, painting, architecture, industrial design, fashion, interior design, and computer arts. When your child becomes involved in visual arts he has embarked on a marvelous journey, rich with history and filled with adventure. Your child will find that his interest in art will provide him with enough different challenges to last the rest of his life.

Your child's deep and sincere love for art will grow with your support. A successful parent is one who provides and nurtures the interests and abilities in his child. When a child is allowed to do the thing he loves, he is following his inclination, his talents. He will be at peace with himself. When your child displays to you very early a love and passion for art, it is important for you not to ignore it. It is my hope that the information found in this book will provide you with the tools to help your children be successful in art, whether it be as a hobby or as a profession.

What the world needs is not romantic lovers who are sufficient unto themselves, but husbands and wives who live in communities, relate to other people, carry on useful work and willingly give time and attention to their children.
Margaret Mead, in *Redbook* magazine, November 1965.

1.

TALENTED IN ART

The words "talented in art" can be best understood if you first realize that a talent can be innate or acquired. Some people will become talented artists because they have carefully and diligently studied all aspects of art and have a strong desire to succeed at it. Other people just seem to manifest their talent naturally. Whether your child is naturally talented or talented because she works hard at it, that talent then must be developed to the point where she produces accomplished works of art before she can truly be called "talented in art."

The word "talent," according to the *Random House College Dictionary*, is:

Talent: "A special natural ability or aptitude, a capacity for achievement or success ...;

Ability: Competence in an activity, special skills, a word for mental power, native or acquired, enabling one to do things well ...;

Aptitude: Readiness in learning, innate or acquired capacity for something ...;

Achievement: Something accomplished, as by superior ability or special effort."

According to the dictionary, your child is talented in art if she has special skills, native or acquired, that enable her to do her artwork well; if she readily learns art skills; and if she is capable of producing accomplished artwork.

COMMON CHARACTERISTICS OF A TALENTED CHILD

While teaching art in the public schools, I have noticed that many of the students who show artistic talent have similar behavioral characteristics. Most of them:

- enjoy working with their hands
- respond with great interest to the way the world around them looks, for example the colors in a sunset, the way a street curves along the landscape, or pictures and drawings in magazines and textbooks
- are very serious about their own artwork
- are very eager to study new art materials and books
- love new art projects
- have friends who tell them they are better at art than anyone else their age
- usually spend free time in class doing art-related activities

In each classroom of approximately twenty-five students, there would almost always be at least two or three children who displayed a talent in art. I also found that there were at least five students in each room who showed artistic potential, but because of their lack of confidence or proper support from home or school most of them never developed it.

TALENT IS FAITH IN ONE'S ABILITIES

While teaching art to both talented and not-so-talented children in the public school system, I noticed that new art projects would cause more than half of the students to tell me, "I have no art talent, how do you expect me to do that?!" Many of these students felt defeated from that first day in kindergarten when they saw how well some of their classmates could draw. They gave up too soon. By the time they reached second grade, their "I can'ts" became a self-fulfilling prophecy. Because these students had given up long before, they never practiced their drawing skills. You could say they lost faith in themselves. So, if faith in oneself is that crucial, it should always be fostered and never undermined.

Some children need nurturing and encouragement to develop

enough faith in themselves to learn how to create art. An artist has an incredible task ahead when she is given a blank piece of paper or a lump of clay. To help her you might say, "You can do it. It may be hard, but you have done hard things before. I feel sure you'll be able to do it, and with a little practice it may turn out better than you ever dreamed possible." Or perhaps, "Remember the picture of the horse that you drew last week? This one you did yesterday is even better. You drew the top part of his back legs much larger than the front, just like they are on real horses. I think your dad and I will soon have one good enough to get professionally framed." With positive, uplifting statements running through your child's mind, she will have confidence in her abilities and be better able to face the formidable task of creating something from nothing.

When you say to your child, "You can do better than that," you shame her. When she is proud of herself, she will set higher goals. If you are ashamed of her, she may feel ashamed too. Keep your goals in mind with your child and foster her talent with encouraging, positive words. When the one person in the world who knows her best thinks she can do it, then maybe she *can* learn the new art skill.

Even the best of artists will experience times when they lose faith in their abilities. When this happens to your child, remind her that faith in herself is what got her where she is today, and that same faith will help her get where she wants to go.

It generally happens that assurance keeps an even pace with ability.
Samuel Johnson, The Rambler (1750-52)

TALENT AND THE ABILITY TO DRAW

One of the misconceptions about the word "talent" is that if a person can draw, she is talented in art. Talent, in order for it to have its full meaning, has to go beyond ability to the actual production of quality artworks. For example, the ability to draw well is not necessarily linked to talent. Betty Edwards, in her book, *Drawing on the Artist Within*, tells us that she can teach people to draw in a matter of months just by teaching them how to *see* in a manner suitable to drawing. The ability to draw is basically a skill that can be taught to anyone, like reading or math.

Just as you wouldn't say a person who knows how to read is talented in reading, you should not assume that a person who can draw is talented in art. There are many other factors to be considered; for instance, does your child have a constant desire to learn more about drawing or other forms of art? Without that drive, she won't develop her skills into an art talent—all she has is an ability to draw.

HARD WORK PLUS TALENT

No amount of time or money can make a child have the desire to develop a skill into a talent. One of my sons is good at music, but he is unwilling to work at it. His father worked very hard at his piano-playing and by the age of sixteen, he was recognized as a young man who was very talented in music. Our son learned Suzuki violin and became very proficient at it by the time he was eight. He had great potential for becoming a talented musician like his father. However, as he reached the age of ten, he lost interest and desire, eventually giving up his interest in music altogether. We spent a lot of time and money trying to rekindle this potential talent. Until he is willing to put in the necessary effort, his talent will lie dormant.

To call my son talented would be a disservice to his father and all the other talented musicians who have worked hard and continue to work hard at maintaining their status. The most I can say about my son is that he has a potential for music if he ever cares to work hard at it.

T alent is a question of quantity. Talent does not write one page:
it writes three hundred.
Jules Renard, Journal (1887)

INTEREST IN ART BUT NO TALENT

Artistic talent comes easily for some; for others it may take a lot of hard work; for some it may never come at all. Before you give up on one of your children who clearly shows no artistic potential, remember that an *interest* in art is just as important in our world as the talent itself.

Those who have a deep interest in art in general but don't actually produce quality artwork provide a vital network for the support of talented artists. There are also art-related careers that require a love of art but not necessarily an ability to produce it.

Our public schools teach music and art not just to single out the talented but to encourage and develop an interest and appreciation of them. I was never talented in music, but I've always enjoyed listening to it. My love for music made my parents think I had music potential, but after years of practice, I clearly showed no musical talent. My love for music and many years of lessons gave me enough knowledge to enjoy it at a variety of levels.

If your child loves art, but never quite gets good at it, do not discourage her. She may use it as a hobby, incorporate her love of art in one of the many art-related careers where art production is not necessary, or be a patron of the arts.

Art as a hobby can be categorized in two areas: collecting and creating. A hobby is something you do just for fun. Hobbies provide an outside interest, are relaxing, encourage friendships, build work habits, stimulate learning, and sometimes even develop into a part-time business. If your child enjoys doing art and does not want to put in the hard work it takes to become a professional, art, in any form, makes an interesting and a fulfilling hobby.

PROVEN TALENT

The truly talented artists are in the art museums and better art galleries throughout the world. Having a picture in a local gallery or fair does not mean that the artist is talented in art. She may be a potential artist, still struggling with that long learning process necessary to get to a level of artistic competence it takes to be called talented.

When you purchase art created by an artist who has great potential, you are encouraging her to continue developing her skills. If people only bought artwork by the truly talented artists, it would be very difficult for those who are developing their talent to survive financially and emotionally. With a strong desire, a lot of hard work, and support from others, a potentially talented artist may eventually gain recognition.

PROBLEMS ASSOCIATED WITH BEING TALENTED

Being artistically talented is often difficult for a young child because she is in some ways different from her peers. For example, she is probably one of the few kids in her class who can draw well and may be given "hero" status. A second grade boy named Chris drew wonderfully funny cartoons that were treasured by his classmates; they would even fight over the ones he threw in the trash. Linda was so good at drawing that her friends would rather watch her draw than they would do their own work. Darek, a seventh grader, drew airplanes that were of such professional quality that his friends bought them. Each of these students was a kind of hero to many of their classmates. If you have been told this about your child, remember that this happens to many artistic children.

When being put on a pedestal bothers your child, you might explain that this is normal for children who are better at art than their friends. If it is making her feel a little too "special," you might enroll her in an art class where there are a lot of other talented children.

Another problem that you may see in your child is that she gets so carried away with her interest in art that she forgets her friends and family. This may cause hurt feelings and could cause problems with her relationships with her friends. Sometimes she may even forget to eat or sleep. These problems usually correct themselves. When I was in college I met a nineteen-year-old girl who had to be reminded to eat all her meals. She would work so hard at her art projects that her level of concentration would mask her hunger pains. Her friends knew this and would be sure she got her meals. When I taught school, my airplane artist Darek received a new aircraft book for his eleventh birthday and brought it to school to study in his free time. After staying in for recess for three days in a row, his friends told him that was enough. They wanted Darek to go outside and play with them. When your child's passion for art interferes with her normal daily living for long periods of time, you may have to step in and remind her that life is at its best when it is balanced with hard work and play.

Another problem artistic children face is ridicule. If she comes to you upset because her classmates laugh at her, remind her that this happens to people who are different than the majority of people. This difference, if cultivated, will ultimately bring her success and great satisfaction. As Sydney Smith stated:

Whatever you are from nature, keep to it; never desert your own line of talent. Be what nature intended you for, and you will succeed; be anything else, and you will be ten thousand times worse than nothing!

LABELING A CHILD AS TALENTED

The word "talented" should probably not be used around young children. Labeling a child as being gifted or talented is very hard for the child to understand. When my granddaughter asked me what it meant when a teacher told her she had talent, I said, "They are trying to tell you that you have a special ability and interest. Each one of us has at least one special ability. It's that part of someone you remember best. Linda can read well, Joany's hair and clothes are always so neat and perfect, Jeff can really draw horses. Your special ability is creating art; we all enjoy your work. It is your responsibility to take that special difference, develop it as best you can, and then find a way that you can use it to make our world a better place while you are young and when you are older. Some of your friends are talented in art, some in reading, while others have a talent for being warm and friendly. When she said you are talented in art, she was telling you how much she enjoyed your artwork." The word "talent" is very hard for a young child to comprehend. She might better understand it if you just say how much and why you enjoy her artwork.

HARD WORK AND TALENT

Talent goes beyond ability to encompass hard work. For your child to be successful, she must work hard at developing and maintaining her art skills. Some people thought to have talent in school fail in the working world because they don't know how to work hard. If learning and creating art comes easily for your child, she must learn to work hard, too. It would be a shame if a very talented artist lost her job because she was not willing to do the work.

For an artistically talented person to work at a job totally unrelated to art would be a loss to us all. My late husband graduated from Hershey School for Boys back in the 1950s and always talked about a talented math student who would continually score higher than everyone else in mathematics tests, and no one ever saw him study. What he learned was strictly during class. By his senior year he was clearly the most talented math student in the whole class. At their twenty-fifth class reunion, my husband found out this math genius was driving a truck, had been divorced several times, and was drinking heavily. Everyone at the reunion was very surprised—they had fully expected him to work at a place like NASA. He may have been talented in math in the '50s, but he definitely cannot carry this title today. We found out that when he got into college, he found other mathematically talented students, and rather than working hard to keep up with them, he gave up. If your child is talented in art, you need to challenge her continually and encourage her ability to work hard. Life is not easier because you are talented—it still requires hard work to be successful.

Continually challenge your child by exposing her to other artistically talented people early in her studies. Impress upon her that her natural artistic ability may get her a job, but it will take hard work to keep it. She may get a commission to paint a mural on an old building, but it will take many long, hard hours of designing, painting, researching a theme, getting the proper materials, and then painting it before she gets paid. How well it is done will also determine whether she will get another commission.

Some kids have an unlimited ability and desire to work hard; others need guidance. If your child needs help learning how to work hard, you can encourage her with positive reinforcement. You might say, "You worked very hard on this picture. The extra time you spent on it gave it a new quality I haven't seen in any of your other work." Consider your child's level of ability to work hard and then strengthen it often with positive reinforcement. When talent and hard work go hand in hand they usually equal success.

2.

ART LESSONS

Art lessons can be given individually or to a group. The most common type is group lessons. Local art leagues usually offer art lessons for children and young adults taught by their members. You can also find classes in community centers, at colleges and universities, and in the art museums of larger cities. If you cannot find an art teacher, ask your local reference librarian to assist you.

PRIVATE LESSONS

Private art lessons are usually more expensive than group lessons, but you may feel the advantages outweigh the cost. When your child is the only student, the teacher is no longer involved with the needs of the group and can concentrate all his energy and knowledge on the one student.

Our kids are so used to institutions that private lessons might make some of them feel uncomfortable. On the other hand, they might be just what your child needs — individualized attention. Kaye, one of my second grade art students, felt that she wanted extra help with her artwork. She asked me if I could give her private lessons, but because I lived too far away, I told her to ask a local artist. As her art teacher, I was with her class forty-five minutes a week; individually I was able to help her two to three minutes per class. Kaye and I discussed group art classes, but she preferred a private tutor. A local artist was found and within three sessions, they were comfortable with each other and very happy. When giving your child private art lessons, he may benefit more by changing his tutor every six months or year if possible.

The cost of private lessons is usually high, but almost all artists have worked many years refining their skills, just like any professional, and appreciate getting paid well. To keep the cost down, you might consider private lessons in groups of six sessions, two or three times a year. Private lessons are a wonderful way for your child to get to know a real, practicing artist.

GROUP LESSONS

Art lessons in a group are exciting for many students. One of the biggest advantages is that your child will get to meet other students who love art. This can be very comforting to a child who has always felt different from his classmates. As the class progresses, he will probably find himself learning not only from the teacher but from his peers. Group lessons in a museum or college will give your child a chance to view a collection of fine art. Group art instruction usually runs in sessions of six to eight weeks.

Many children find this the best kind of art class because they enjoy the competitiveness of being in a group; they can learn more by watching others; they become less self-conscious about their own work; they develop new friends who love art too; and they understand better how to make their artwork communicate to others.

The size of the group is very important. Your child will best be taught if he is in a group no larger than ten students.

NO OUTSIDE INSTRUCTION

Some children do not want any outside instruction. They are perfectly happy working on their own. I was like that when I was very young. Going to school was more structured activity than I wanted, so to go to another structured activity was out of the question. In teaching school, I have also found this to be true of some of my best artists. They enjoyed learning on their own, at their own pace, and quite honestly, they did quite well. A little help from me once a week was plenty.

If your child does not want instruction from lessons, provide plenty of informative books. Questions will come up that he will need answers to, and if he has ready access to books containing this information, he can learn the new skills while his curiosity is at its peak. You can find art books at fund-raising book sales put on by your library or community group, in book stores, and in libraries. If you cannot find a particular book, the reference librarian can do a computer search through all the libraries in their system and find it for you. If you want to purchase a book, the larger book stores can find it for you too. Information about the area of interest should be readily available to your child so he can learn about it while his interest is at its peak. A good art library of his own will be very helpful to your child.

If your child tells you he doesn't want art lessons, you probably shouldn't push him. Let him know you would be willing to give him private or group art lessons, but you realize it is up to him. A visit to a class in session will sometimes help a child determine whether he wants to attend.

Art instruction is not absolutely necessary, especially in this age where information is so readily available, but lessons will speed up his movement from one state of skill development to another and expose him to other artists like himself. Many children enjoy private and group lessons, but others feel their art is their own private world and they like it that way.

CONSULTATION

Art instruction can also be given on a consulting basis. This is when your child receives instruction from his art teacher only by request. Consultations are a good way for a child to receive instruction when he does not want private or group art lessons but realizes that he needs some help once in a while.

This is a relatively new concept and finding a teacher may be difficult. You could begin your search by writing a letter to your local art league explaining the kind of instruction your child needs, and ask if there is an artist available who would be willing to teach your child on a consulting basis, and if so, what the fee would be.

IN SUMMARY

There are many pros and cons to giving your child art lessons. Try to give your child at least one art class experience, even if he feels he doesn't want to take classes. Many potentially talented children are shy, especially about their artwork, and will choose not to attend a class because they are easily frightened. Exposure to other artistic children, even for a short period of time, will give your child more confidence and reassurance in his abilities.

If your child is the best artist in his grade and has no competition, he may need to be put in an art class where he is not the best. Billy, one of my talented second graders, was "Mr. King" to his classmates, until he met the new boy, Chris. After Billy was dethroned as "the best 'drawer' in the whole world," he decided maybe this Chris fellow could teach him how to draw better. Besides that, he concluded, if he worked really hard, he would then draw better than Chris and could be "top banana" again. By the end of the year the two were good friends, and Billy found out that being the best was not as important as having a friend who loved drawing too. Art classes give your child a chance to develop friendships with other artistic children that will enhance his abilities and give him humility. The competition and stimulation of a good art class will encourage his talent and help keep alive his desire to work hard at his art skills.

If your child needs the stimulation of a good teacher and other art students, has asked for art lessons, and is willing to sacrifice the time, you might seriously consider giving him art lessons. They can begin as early as seven years old, last from three weeks to one year, or they can even be in the form of a summer art camp. Art lessons are not necessary to developing your child's artistic talent, but they are a good idea once every year or two.

3.

ENCOURAGING YOUR CHILD

For your child to create at his maximum potential, he will need some encouragement. The most influential support will come from the people he most respects and loves—his family. Encouragement is vital to your child's success because without it, he may lose interest in art. To help you, I have included in this chapter some ideas that I have used with my art students and my own children.

THINGS YOU CAN DO TO ENCOURAGE YOUR CHILD

Your child will need a special place to do his artwork. When my sister left for college, my parents gave me her bedroom for my art studio. I was so excited with their gift that within a short period of time, I had created a painting that was good enough to frame. To give up a small area of your home for your child to develop his talent is an act of loving generosity and real encouragement.

Encouragement can also be given through making sure he has enough art supplies. You do not need to get everything he wants, but be sure he has some basic art supplies.

Another thing you can do to encourage your child is to have a lot of paintings and sculptures in your home. These can be in the form of limited edition prints, figurines, original paintings, crafts, sculptures, mobiles, photographs, and reproductions of famous paintings (some libraries have these to loan to their patrons). To keep your child noticing your collection, try moving the pieces from room to room. The owl I purchased in Brown County, Indiana has been in every room of my house and he looks a little different in each room. A very inexpensive way to have quality art in your home is to use reproductions of paintings found in art magazines, old books, and even on postcards. You can tape them on a wall or put them in an inexpensive frame. By having your home full of artwork, you will be encouraging your child to "give it a try" too.

An occasional reward enhances a child's desire to continue improving his art skills. The reward need not be expensive. Notice what your child has been working on for the past several days. Say, for example, if he's been drawing a lot of horses, you might look for a picture of a horse. They are on greeting cards and calendars and in newspapers and magazines. You might even buy him a horse figurine. A reward is also a good way to get your child out of an unproductive or "fallow" period. The stimulation may help him get back at his artwork. The reward is best if it is not in the form of a bribe. For example, a bribe might be worded as follows, "If you draw me a picture and clean up your art corner, we'll all go out for hamburgers." Although this will probably work, it usually has only short-term effects. You may even find you have to bribe him more often than you are willing. Give your child an unexpected reward once in a while to show him just how pleased you are with his interest in art.

Entering your child's artwork in a contest, in my opinion, is usually not the way to encourage him. I have seen too many very talented young artists get passed by when judges were handing out ribbons. The winner of the foot race is much easier to determine than the best artist in a contest. There are many factors involved. The problem is usually not with your child's artwork but with the judges. I suggest you do not allow your child to enter competitions unless you are willing to sit down and discuss what *not winning* really means, and you are willing to take the time to check out the judges to see if they are truly qualified to judge children's art.

The first big encouragement for me was when my mother had one of my paintings professionally framed. If at all possible, frame your child's work and hang it where everyone can enjoy it. If you would like to set off a sculpture, it can be mounted on a nice piece of wood. This kind of recognition will give your child confidence that someday he just might be a "professional" artist. Although professional framing is expensive, you will probably need to do this only once for your child.

Another way to encourage your child is to take him to the library. He may want to check out art books, or he may want to check out a book on a specific subject like horses, flowers, or cars. The adult section of the library has books that your child can enjoy too, but you may want to check these books for inappropriate material. The easiest way to find art-related books is to ask the librarian or look for books with catalog numbers in the 700-780 range. Books give your child a chance to learn new techniques and expand visual awareness.

At some point, someone will probably offer to pay your child for his artwork. It is probably best to accept the payment. When I was in a graduate level art class, the students were asked to tell one of their most encouraging moments. Many said it was the day someone gave them money for their artwork. One girl told of a waitress giving her two dollars for a small drawing she did on a napkin. Another told of her principal offering her money for a painting of a vase of flowers. So please do not say no when money is offered. Your child has worked hard at developing his skill and can always use the money to purchase more art supplies.

Let your child help in areas of running the house where art skills are involved. Here are a few ideas:

- selection of wallpaper, drapes, furniture, bedspreads, etc.
- rearranging furniture
- making a garage sale sign
- making name tags, banners, hats for a special event
- designing cards to send to family and friends
- help in selection of houseplants and designing next year's garden
- making a calendar for the family
- making a toy for a young child
- setting the dinner table in an attractive manner
- designing and sewing pillows for the couch
- being responsible for maintaining and supplying a vase of fresh flowers in the house
- letting him be the photographer or video-camera operator, if he is old enough

The suggestions above will allow your child to put his art skills to use in a practical way. It will also open up new ideas for possible careers or hobbies.

Your artistic child does not need you to do a lot, but he does need some support and encouragement. This can be in the form of hanging pictures in your home, giving him rewards, and providing him with a good selection of books. Remember, it is ultimately up to him. Be patient with your child, encourage him, but do not push or cajole. He will move from one learning stage to another when he is ready. As a wonderful nun told me once, we open the doors for our children, but it's up to them to walk in.

THINGS YOU CAN SAY TO ENCOURAGE YOUR CHILD

What we say to our children is just as important as what we do. Take a few minutes to talk to him about his artwork. Your child has probably come up to you with his picture and said, "Mom, Dad, what do you think?" and you replied, "Yes, isn't this nice, you did a great job!" You probably wanted to say more but were unsure what to say. Here are a few ideas.

When talking to your child about his artwork, speak with compassion. Tell him that you understand how very hard it is to look at a dog and then draw it. If you notice that he has, for example, made the dog's legs too long, mention to him that one of the hardest things about drawing animals is getting their body parts in the right proportions. You might then talk about how some dogs like Basset Hounds, Dachshunds, and Welsh Corgis have very short legs in comparison to their bodies. You have not offered advice or criticism. What you have done is offered sympathy and understanding for the complexity of his task. He realizes mistakes are good because each time he makes one he learns something, and mistakes are nothing for which he should be embarrassed. A cute example is with my little first graders. "Oops!" I'd say, "You forgot their feet and shoes. It sure is hard to draw shoes." With a smile and a giggle, each would happily return to his desks ready to accept the new challenge. Before class was over, the people in their pictures would have feet and beautiful shoes too. With compassionate encouragement, your child will eagerly return to his artwork. He may even say to himself, "Art is hard and I do make mistakes. I'm glad Mom and Dad understand. But you know, because I drew my dog's legs too long, I learned to look at a dog's shape a little closer. And mistakes aren't quite as embarrassing now that I know Mom and Dad make them too." When the people your child loves the most show him tender understanding of the immense complexity of his art-related endeavors, he will not become discouraged by his mistakes.

One of the easiest things to talk about is color. Tell him about the colors you like. For example, you might tell your child that the soft blue he used reminds you of a shirt that you like to wear in the spring. You can even talk about how colors make you feel—blues or greens make us feel cool and calm; reds and yellows, vibrant and warm. Most of the time a child will choose his colors without thinking. A junior high student of mine was given an assignment to draw her favorite animal. She chose to draw a horse that lived on her farm. When she drew the horse, she colored it bright red. When I asked her about it, she said, "Oh, no, my horse isn't red, she's pure black." An artist can change what he sees in order to communicate his message. Without realizing it, my student, through the use of the color red, told us how much she loved her horse. Talking about color can encourage your child to use it more effectively.

Talk about the recognizable objects in his picture. For example, if your child draws a teddy bear sitting on a bed, you might ask him if it's his teddy bear, or is it his friend's? Your discussion may also lead to your telling him a story about teddy bears. He may want to tell you one too. My boys' grandmother used to use their pictures as a springboard to telling her tales of what happened to her in "the good old days," when she was a "weeee little girl" living on an Oklahoma farm. Through talking about the things your child has put in his picture, he will soon realize that everything in his picture is important.

Your child will also need some encouragement with his skills or techniques. You may know very little about art or you may know a lot. The most important thing is to notice if your child needs help. If he keeps making the same mistake over and over again, you might step in and offer suggestions. For example, you can tell him he needs to change his water more often so the colors in his painting will not get muddy-looking. If you do not know how to help him or if you notice he is struggling too long, you will need to get him some help. You can use the library or get help from a local artist. Most art skills and techniques can be self-taught through studying other artists' works and through reading, but a good teacher can be an invaluable asset to a child's progress, especially in the area of art skills and techniques.

Trusting your child sometimes means saying nothing at all. Art is an area where your child will be working on his own most of the time. He will be progressing at his own speed. There will even be times when he is not working at all, and this is normal. Say nothing, just trust him. When he is ready, he will be back at it. He may even get back to his artwork with deeper concentration than ever before. But if this slack period lasts longer than you think it should (one or two months), place items he likes to draw around the house. Art is a quiet activity. He will need others to comment on his work and assist him occasionally, but most of the time your child needs to be left alone to think and reflect on what he is creating.

Talk to your child when he is unsure about his artwork. As your child is learning to create, he will often be concerned that his artwork doesn't look right. Your job, as his parent, is first to deal with his concern. He is feeling mixed up and this may worry him. I have found the best way to help is with reassurance. I would tell about the times when I felt confused too. The next thing you need to deal with is why he doesn't like his artwork. If he feels that it doesn't look right, it is probably so. There is a certain "click" in your mind, when your artwork is right. In the three examples that follow, I will first tell you how I handled the worry my son felt because he had never been unsure with his artwork before, and then I will tell you how I used confusion to improve not only his artwork but his skills.

When my child brought me his latest painting and said he liked it but something wasn't quite right, I said to him, "Whenever I shop for new clothes, it is hard for me to make up my mind which items I want to purchase. This is especially true when it comes to buying my shoes. In fact, it usually takes me about two weeks to find a pair that I really like. Do you remember my winter boots? It took me two years to find them and a lot of winters with two and three pairs of socks under my old ones! But the funny thing was, when I did find them, I knew right away that they were the right pair."

When teaching embroidery, a student was confused about which colors of embroidery thread he should use in his project. He asked me, "Do these colors go together?" I said, "If you don't know whether the colors are compatible, they probably are not. Each of us has his own color preference, so it's best if I do not help you. If you aren't sure, you need to try some others. You will know when all the colors go together. When it's right, it's right and you know it."

My mother, who was an oil painter, and I loved to talk about the paintings she wasn't sure about. First, we would look at the colors. If they were okay, we would then start looking at the rest of the painting. We would look for lines, objects, shapes that could be eliminated without losing her painting's message. I would hold my hand over an area, then she would look at it and see if it should be eliminated. When she found a portion of her oil painting that she felt could be eliminated, she would hold her hand over it and see if I agreed. If we agreed she would change it (sometimes she would change it even though I didn't agree!). After our short talks, her spirits would be high and she would continue working on her painting until she was happy with it.

When your child comes to you unsure of his picture, he usually knows that something is wrong. Reassure him that his confusion will help him be a better artist because he will not be content until it is right. If he cannot find the answer, tell him to hang it on his wall for a few days and see if the answer will come to him. When your child comes to you with mixed-up feelings about his artwork, reassure him that this same thing happens to you, and perhaps this unsettled feeling about his artwork will help him keep working until he is happy with it. The words "I can't" should be avoided. If your child says this to you, assure him that nothing is impossible. Whatever you are trying to learn may be hard, but there is nothing you can't do if you set your mind to it. A child has an incredible amount of art to learn and a lot of it is totally new. Adults need to remember this and be sympathetic and supportive when life's challenges seem overwhelming. Your child will be better able to meet new challenges if he doesn't say words like "I can't." Think of it this way. The words "I can't" lock the doors, and the words "It's hard" leave the door slightly ajar, creating curiosity and challenge.

CONSTRUCTIVE PRAISE

Praise is often difficult to put into words. When working with my students, I found that the standard phrase, "You did a wonderful job," wasn't enough. There was always the look on their faces begging me to tell them more. So I began complimenting them on their accomplishments. Here are a few samples:

"Now that's interesting, you put someone on the horse. Is that you?"

"Good for you, you used the whole paper."

"Your family is all dressed up for church and look at your mother's beautiful shoes."

"The colors you used in the sky are grays and dark blues. It looks as though it is about to rain."

"You know, this picture reminds me of my own house ..."

"You want me to have it? Thank you. I especially like the way you gave her such long, curly hair."

"Your colors are so bright and lively they make me feel excited and cheerful."

"This is the best drawing of a horse that I have seen you do, you even put a bridle on her. I'd like to hang it up."

Words you should try to avoid saying to your child are those that praise his personality. For example:

"You're such a good boy."

"You truly are a talented young man for your age."

"Wonderful, son, you are the greatest."

These are not realistic statements, and the child knows it. Praise what he has actually done, and he will know it is true. Remember, your child will probably be repeating what you told him over and over again. If you have concentrated your praise on what he has done he'll be saying things to himself like, "I did make the sky gloomy, I did make everyone in my family handsome. She really loves my horse picture, I wonder if it's because I've been practicing drawing horses from my new library book." If your praise is about his personality, he may say things like this to himself, "Mom says I am good, I do try to be good, but I am bad sometimes. Yesterday I got so mad at my brother I wanted to break his new bike. And then she told me I was 'talented' in art. What does the word talented mean anyway?" If you are specific in your praise, he will understand why you like his work and be encouraged to use this information in his next project.

CRITICISM

Criticism, in my opinion, is a negative statement and is not to be used when you are trying to encourage your child. If outside criticism bothers your child, talk to him about what was actually said about his artwork. For example, another child may have said, "You can't draw, look at the way you drew that house, and teacher said you're talented in art." This is very discouraging for a child to hear. Talk to him about the first statement, "Can he draw?" Then the second, "Do you feel you could have drawn a better house?" Talk about how children did that to you when you were young too. Soon he will realize that although most of what his friends criticized him for was untrue, some of it was true: "Perhaps I didn't draw that house right." If you need to criticize, do it in a positive, encouraging manner. Constructive criticism has no negative comments — it just states what was to be done and tells you how to do it. Destructive criticism creates doubt, self-condemnation, and distrust of others. Here is an example:

One of my kindergarten students drew the all-familiar house on the hill scene. One of her peers gave constructive criticism when she said, "Your house is in the sky. You need to put land around it so the people can get inside." Another peer gave her destructive criticism when he said, "That's a house?! Houses can't fly! Look at this, guys." The first criticism told her she did have a problem, but it also told her what had to be done. The second comment made her feel inadequate and humiliated in front of her friends. To encourage your child in his artwork, try to limit criticism, and if it is necessary be sure it is constructive.

To encourage your child, look for what he has done well and talk about it. Say it to your child loud and clear. Most adults and children rarely receive verbal positive reinforcement. The only time they hear a remark is when they are doing something that needs correction. When your child has succeeded in communicating his message, tell him so. Give him a pat on the back, a firm handshake, a smile, or a hug. These small gestures coupled with the suggestions stated in this chapter will give your child the courage to develop his abilities in art.

In this chapter, I talked about things you can do to encourage your child in his search for excellence in art. Your child needs a private place to work, some supplies, other artists' works to view, an occasional reward, and books to study. He will also need to talk to you about his artwork in a positive, motivating way. Your words should concentrate on what he has done and not on him personally. Children are not capable of providing all of their own motivation and encouragement. It is up to all of us as parents, grandparents, family, friends, and teachers to help him until he is old enough to encourage himself.

4.

ART TERMINOLOGY

Your child will be talking about her art projects in a way that may at first seem confusing. She will probably talk about the elements of art and the principles of design. Just as other professions have their special terms, so does art. An *element of art* is a term used to mean a basic component or symbol of art. A work of art will contain all or some of these elements: line, value, shape, form, space, color, and texture. A *principle of design* is a guide or rule by which the elements are placed in an artwork to make it easy to look at or to give it a certain effect. The principles of design are rhythm, balance, proportion, variety, emphasis, and unity. As your child develops her art skills she will be talking about elements and how well she has used the principles of design.

A good understanding of the words used by artists will help your child improve her artwork and will help her enjoy looking at fine art. When my husband first went with me to art museums, he was bored after we were there only fifteen minutes. When I told him that each artist takes the symbols and rules and uses them to help communicate ideas, he suddenly started to take more interest in each picture. He didn't realize that artists had rules. The Picasso that looked like a child's drawing of a woman crying became more interesting as I explained what it meant: "Picasso had a choice of using thick or thin lines to outline her face. He chose thick lines to depict the boldness of her tears. The eyes are the first thing you see when you look at the picture, which is called *emphasis*. Eyes are said to be the window to one's soul, so Picasso is telling you that the tears flowing from them are telling you something very deep and personal about this lady, and they are the most important part of this picture. The eyes are both drawn off center, which makes you feel almost as upset as the person in the picture." As he ventured through the museum on his own, he found that art was indeed very exciting. Now that he understood the rules artists follow, he was able to enjoy it. You too may find more enjoyment of not only the master artists' but your child's work, as you read and understand the meaning of the terms listed below.

When an artist creates she makes many choices. She decides whether to use thick or thin lines, bright or dull colors, or large or small shapes. When you study a work of art, see if you can understand why the artist made each decision. Discuss artwork in terms of the elements of art and principles of design with your child and help her understand their importance in her work too.

ELEMENTS OF ART

COLOR—This is one of the most important elements of art. Color can be used by an artist not only to describe the way an object looks but to express a mood. The color red can be used to depict excitement, blue is used for sadness, green for envy, yellow for cowardice, or purple for royalty. A picture using all dark, dull colors will give you a different feeling than one with light, bright ones.

Artists will often take the actual color of an object and change it to help communicate the message. If the artist wanted to tell you that the man in her painting was a king, she might use purple in his skin tones. If she wanted to show an extremely unhappy lady, she might use a lot of blue. To take this idea a little further, the artist can show a woman who was warm and friendly by using reds; one who loves gardening in greens; or a cowardly woman in yellow.

FORM—When the object has form, it has three dimensions—length, width, and depth. People, buildings, and flowers are just a few of the many forms around us. Shape and form are similar terms except that when a form is depicted it shows another dimension—depth. A circle shape is made into the form of a ball or sphere by shading.

LINE—A mark that is longer in length than in breadth. It may be long, short, wavy, zigzag, or any way you can imagine. We see lines all around us in writing, trees, clouds, buildings, and even in a line of people. Some say a line is like a dot making its path through space. In a work of art, line can be used to control the eye movement of the viewer. In some of the landscapes of the old masters you will see a road in the lower lefthand corner of the picture winding to the back right corner and then angling a little to the left. Landscape artists will sometimes use a road as a line that leads the viewer into the picture.

The way the line is drawn can also give it meaning—a diagonal line shows action, a horizontal line depicts calmness or quiet, lines spreading from a center show overflowing life or a bursting of activity, circular lines show a holding inside or a unity of whatever they define. The way an artist uses lines in a picture can determine its mood.

SHAPE—Each object that you see has a shape. An apple is a different shape than a tree, and your eye is a different shape than your hand. A shape has two dimensions—length and width. Some common shapes are circle, rectangle, triangle, oval, and hexagon. You might think of a shape as being a silhouette of an object or an outline.

SPACE—The area around or within a form or shape is called space. It is just as important as the object itself because it defines the shape. Negative space is the area around an object, and positive space is the area within an object. When the negative space is large you might have a feeling of loneliness. For example, in a painting of a farmer standing in a large wheat field, the positive shape of his body would be small in comparison to the large negative shape of the wheat field that surrounded it. The artist used negative space to tell us that the farmer feels very lonely as he works in his field.

TEXTURE—The surface of objects feels a certain way, and artists call this texture. It may be rough, smooth, slick, dull, or prickly. When an artist depicts a person, the texture of the hair, skin, and clothing are done in such a way that the person looking at the picture or sculpture knows, without a doubt, what each part of the picture feels like. An artist can show the texture of an object with color or lines. Because we associate certain textures with certain objects, an artist will use texture to create a desired feeling in her artwork. We know that hair feels soft, smooth, and warm, that needles feel prickly and can hurt, and that highly polished metal feels cool and slick. An artist may want to show a person of low moral character by using rough, coarse textures for her skin.

Many children fail to put texture in their pictures. Texture is an important part of our life and should therefore be an important part of their artwork. Talk with your child about the way objects feel; the bark on a tree, a flower petal, the grass under her feet. If she does not know how to put this in her artwork, have her examine other artwork to see how other artists did it. Many of my young students finally understood what I meant by texture when I showed them how to color grass. Most of them would use their crayons in a left to right movement. I pointed out to them that grass grows up, and when I showed them how to draw it in short up and down strokes, using more than one shade of green, they were delighted with the results.

PRINCIPLES OF DESIGN

BALANCE—When an object is in a state of harmony or stability, we say it is in balance. Just as we need balance to walk, we also need it in our artwork so the person looking at our work will feel comfortable. When an artwork is not balanced, people tend to look away.

Balance is found when there is an equal number of things on each side of a design or when a large, heavy object is opposite many smaller ones. Balance is equal distribution of visual weight. Symmetrical balance is when both sides are alike; for example, a butterfly. Asymmetrical balance is when both sides are different, but they still look balanced, as with a tree. An artist may use one large shape and put it with a few small and medium shapes to create balance.

If your child is not sure whether her picture is balanced, have her hold it up to a mirror. Is it heavier on one side than the other?

EMPHASIS—Just as you emphasize a word when you are trying to make a point, a picture should have an emphasis. The emphasis is usually an object but it can be just a color, line, shape, texture, or form. If you wanted to emphasize the happiness of a little girl, you could use a lot of the color red. The emphasis of a picture can also be the focal point. This is the part of the picture you see first; in a still life of apples you might see the one that is cut in half first; in a portrait you may see a young girl's lovely hair; or in a landscape, a boat. What the artist chooses to emphasize is usually what leads you into the picture and encourages you to look at the rest of it.

PROPORTION—This is the size of one part in relation to another. In order for a drawing of a human to appear like a human, it must have the proportions relatively correct. Proportion also refers to the size of one object in relationship to another—a six-inch man cannot comfortably get into a four-inch doorway. An artist can even distort proportions to help convey a message.

RHYTHM—In art, rhythm is a repetition of an element. Because our life is so full of repeated sights and sounds, our art too should have rhythm. It's the reason we find a corn field, a fence, a flock of geese, the stripes on a zebra, or the buildings of a city so visually appealing. Each one is repeated over and over, until you get a sense of rhythm. An art piece has more visual appeal if it has rhythm. An artist can repeat lines, textures, colors, forms, or shapes to create rhythm. Just as our natural world is full of repetition, so should our artwork be.

UNITY—Some think of unity as glue; it is that part of a picture that holds it together. All of the parts of a picture are changed so they are like each other. Sometimes an artist will use color to unify a picture. She may choose to do this by placing a small amount of one color in all the colors. Unity can also be achieved by line. If every line in the entire piece is curved, you could say the artist used line to unify her artwork. This can also be thought of as harmony. Unity can also be achieved by greatly limiting the number of shapes, colors, or lines or by repetition.

VARIETY—Because people do not like to see the same thing for too long, an artist needs to put variety into artwork. She can slightly change the appearance of an object or she can put in its opposite. A picture of a still life is much more interesting if there is a variety of objects. If all the pieces of fruit in a still life are apples, the artist might cut one open for variety.

IN SUMMARY

This all may seem very confusing to you if you are not an artist, but if you familiarize yourself with the terms and rules you will be better able to talk about your child's work with her. These are important concepts for your child to learn. Some artists keep a list of them on their wall for quick reference.

As you develop an understanding of the elements of art and the principles of design, you may find you are enjoying other artists' work more. You will then be better able to understand the whys and hows used to create it. The next time you see a portrait of a lady by Picasso, you can see how he used bold, heavy lines to describe her character. The eyes were off-balance to depict her mood, and Picasso unified the picture by using simple, elementary colors. You may never become an artist yourself, but your child's interest in art may give you a better appreciation of art.

An element of art is a basic component or symbol of art. The *elements of art* are color, form, line, space, shape, and texture.

A principle of design is a guide or rule by which the elements are placed in an artwork to make it easy to look at or give it a certain effect. The *principles of design* are balance, emphasis, proportion, rhythm, unity, and variety.

5.

CAREERS IN ART

Your child is very important not only to you but to the future of this country. As his parent you have probably wondered if he can make a living and a contribution to society with his art skills. There are many careers that need people who are talented in art. This chapter is designed to give you a brief knowledge of some of the jobs your child can pursue as an adult. Each job requires a knowledge of specific art-related skills, as well as a love and an understanding of art. If your child is not sure which career he would like to pursue, he can receive guidance from your local high school or college by taking a vocational interest exam. Children today are fortunate because of the wide variety of careers available to them. After you read the job descriptions, reflect on your child's preferences as he was growing up: is he an organizer; is he interested in reading about other artists; is he more interested in being alone or does he like being around other people?

Working at a job on Saturdays, after school, or in the summer is necessary for some teenagers. If at all possible, try to help your child find a job that is related to his interest in art. Selling will help him understand the complexities of dealing with the public at some point in his career. He might also be a crafts instructor's assistant, work in an arts and crafts store, sell his work in an art/craft fair, help another artist sell at a fair, or even volunteer at a local art museum or art league's gallery. Your child will benefit the most if he uses his free time toward the development of his art skills, through working independently, or through private and group classes. Working is, of course, important for all of us, but if he is to compete in this very competitive world, he will also need a great deal of time to practice and develop his art skills.

This chapter will give you a brief description of some of the more common art-related career. It also gives a list of the many art-related jobs in which your child can use his knowledge of art. More information on each job can be obtained from your local library.

FINE ARTIST

This is the career most people associate with someone who tells you he is an artist. A fine artist can be a painter or sculptor. He works at his art just because he wants to create; there is no practical or useful purpose to his work. Many artists begin this way, but only the courageous remain in a fine art career. Supporting oneself through the sale of fine art is almost impossible. Even the most successful artists have other careers. A sculptor friend of mine told me that money was getting tight for her family, so she had to look for a job. Because of her immense talent, I thought for sure she would do something art-related, but she said, "Actually, Donna, I'm looking for a job as a lab technician's assistant. When I work at a job where I don't have to do a lot of heavy thinking or use my creativity, I am ready to make sculpture when I get home." If your child wants to be a fine artist, you might impress upon him that he will probably need to learn a skill that will supplement his income.

ILLUSTRATOR

An artist who creates drawings and paintings to enhance words is an illustrator. As your child's drawing skills advance, you might notice a style preference. He might enjoy drawing with bright colors, his lines may be all very thick and bold, the eyes on the faces of animals and people are overly large, or he may have a quiet, dreamy feeling in all his work. Most illustrators freelance their work; businesses request work from them. They may draw for advertising companies, book or record covers, children's books, card companies, or even television. A young doctor at my church has a wife who loves to draw. When they first got married, she was so fascinated with the illustrations in his medical publications that she took a few classes in medical illustration. After several years of perfecting her skills, she submitted her drawings to publishers needing medical illustration. After several attempts, she got her first commission and for the past ten years has combined her careers of wife, mother, and illustrator. If you think your child might enjoy a career in illustration, encourage him to learn all he can about other illustrators and commit himself to perfecting his style of drawing or painting.

GRAPHIC DESIGNER

A graphic designer is responsible for the layout of a page before it goes to the printer. He is in charge of choosing the size, shape, and style of the lettering, for the way the letters and illustrations are arranged on the page, and for a certain amount of drawing. All aspects of the appearance of the printed page are the responsibility of the graphic designer. This kind of artist usually works for someone in a regular forty hour a week job. A graphic designer may do the layout for the pages of a magazine or the advertising for a newspaper, create book covers, make posters, design product packaging, plan visuals for a pamphlet, create convention display units, work for an advertising agency in the final layout of their ads, work with computer graphics in a television studio, become an art director for a big corporation, or even design television advertisements.

FABRIC DESIGNER

A fabric designer is in charge of designing not only fabrics for clothing but creating the designs for wall coverings, upholstery, floor coverings, curtains, and even wrapping paper. This is a job in which you are usually hired by a company in the eastern half of the U.S. and work a regular nine-to-five job.

If your child is continually fascinated with fabrics and surface coverings, he might enjoy a career in fabric design. To encourage him, you might get fabric paints and let him make designs on fabrics (shirts, sheets, pillow cases), take him to wallpaper and fabric stores, make a collection of fabric and wallpaper samples he likes, have him design wrapping paper for the family, and let him help choose curtain and upholstery fabrics for your home.

INTERIOR DESIGNER

A career as an interior designer will find your child selecting and choosing furnishings for the interior of a structure. He may choose the carpet for a hotel, help a homeowner purchase and select furniture, assist an architect with the selection of built-in furniture, assist a restaurant owner in color selection of floor and wall covering, select lighting fixtures for a hospital waiting room, or help a bank create an atmosphere of comfort and trust for its customers. An interior designer can run his own business, be an employee of an interior design agency, or work for a large architectural firm.

Your child's interest in interior design can be encouraged by letting him rearrange your furniture, help you choose new household items, work on a doll house, make a photograph collection of many different styles of furnishings, and have a subscription to an interior design magazine.

ARCHITECT

An architect creates buildings. He must understand not only how a building should be constructed but how it will solve the problems of the inhabitants, the best building materials to use, the total cost and how it is related to the client's budget, health and safety restrictions, proper interior maintenance functions, the structure in relationship to the environment and other structures around it, and laws governing its construction.

Landscape architects work with governmental agencies planning highways and parks, are self-employed, and work for corporate clients and homeowners to make the area around a structure beautiful. They need a good working knowledge of trees, shrubs, flowers, and grasses. A landscape architect will also be in charge of designing pathways, fountains, sculptures, walls, and fences. His job is to create an outdoor environment suitable to the building.

To be an architect requires approximately six years of college education. Many architects work for someone, then later open their own business.

Several of my students discovered that they wanted to be architects while making a model home out of cardboard in my eighth grade art class. If your child is interested in architecture, you might take him to the nearest city to look at the interiors and exteriors of new and old buildings, let him watch buildings and homes as they are being torn down or constructed, encourage him to help with home construction projects, purchase how-to construction books to read, let him landscape a specific area of the yard, provide tools and materials for making models and drawings of buildings, keep some books around the house on famous architects, get him a subscription to an architectural magazine, and provide him with an album in which he can collect pictures of architecture that interests him.

INDUSTRIAL DESIGN

An industrial designer takes a product, makes it appealing to the eye, and makes it better. He may be asked to design a chair that offers proper back and leg support, is attractive, and would fit into an interior using furnishings from the early 1920s. Industrial designers work on hard goods and household items like refrigerators, ovens, can openers, clocks, toys, plastic containers, televisions, door knobs, and windows. They also design cars, trucks, office equipment, guns, and computer equipment. Many women are now getting into this once male-dominated industry. Like architecture, advanced education in industrial design is essential.

If you notice that your child is very interested in the way products function and look, even to the point where he is irritated when products are not designed well, he may enjoy a career in industrial design. Talk about the products around your home and in the stores —are they well made, do they function well, are they attractive? Encourage your child to think of ways to improve products around school and home, perhaps even design new and better ones.

PHOTOGRAPHER

Some people think photography is not an art form, but the best photographers all have a good working knowledge of art. The more pictures I take with my camera, the more I appreciate and admire photographers.

There are many careers for photographers including portraiture, advertisements, catalogs, travel, publicity, research, fashion, scientific photography, industrial products and processes, and police records. Full-time photographers are hired by newspapers (photojournalists) and sometimes by large advertising agencies, but most photography work is freelanced. The motion picture industry employs people interested in photography to make films for advertisements, educational instruction, businesses, etc.

If your child is interested in photography, you might get him his own camera with plenty of film and a monthly film developing budget, put him in charge of recording family events, encourage him to collect photographs that he feels are outstanding, take him to photography exhibits, purchase or borrow books about famous photographers, let him create the family calendar with his own photographs, and if you have a video camera let him make a movie.

ART TEACHER

One of the most important art professions is the art teacher, because he trains future artists as well as educating the general public about art. Elementary art teachers instruct children in all the art subjects, while art teachers in high schools usually teach two or three specific media. A teacher in a university can be even more specialized. Teaching takes a great deal of physical, mental, and psychological energy. Some artists can combine a teaching career with freelancing artwork, but many cannot because of the drain on their creativity and the stress. University art professors are not confronted with discipline problems and have the best chance to supplement their income with outside art jobs. A college education is required by all art teachers in the public schools. Teaching is not a career in which you will make a lot of money. However, personally speaking, it is a rewarding career because you get to help others, you are always learning something new, you are making a contribution to the advancement of our society, and you get a lot of unconditional love. If your child admires teachers, loves art, and has always enjoyed explaining things and helping others, he may enjoy a career in teaching art.

ART MUSEUM JOBS

Artists who are mainly interested in art history work in art museums. Museums also hire art teachers for classes and other education concerns, as well as writers and graphic designers to help with brochures and advertisements. If your child enjoys reading art history books and visiting art museums, he may enjoy a career working in an art museum.

CRAFTSPERSON

Today, a person who makes crafts is a lot like a fine artist, except that his items usually serve a purpose. It used to be that a craftsman made one object and then made another exactly the same, but today many craftsmen are studying art in college and becoming aware that the design principles that make a painting or sculpture fine art can also be used in making their crafts. Some craftspeople are still involved in the mass producing of pre-patterned items, but today we also have enlightened crafters who take an idea and use their knowledge of fine art to personalize their work and make it better.

Ceramics (pottery), jewelry, and fabric items are three of the crafts in which an artist can make an item relatively quickly with minimum expense and be able to sell the finished item at a reasonable price. Other crafts like weaving, quilting, embroidery, or wood carving all require a great deal of time to complete each item and therefore are more expensive to create. For example, a potter can make a 10" pot in about twenty minutes with a minimal amount of money spent on supplies. He will be able to sell the pot easily for five times the amount of time and money put into it. A weaver can make a blanket in approximately forty hours. He will have to sell the blanket for three times the amount of time and money he has put into it to receive enough money to make it worth his while. This, of course, makes his item very expensive. Any craft that takes a great deal of time to complete is usually hard to sell because an artist needs to be paid not only for supplies and equipment but for his labor.

A craftsman, like a fine artist, needs another source of income. Some people feel that teaching is a good way to supplement an artist's income, but having been an elementary art teacher myself for many years, I found it next to impossible to work on my art when

I came home. In fact, that was one of the main drawbacks—everyone else got to make artwork but me!

Craftsmen in general, I have found, are supportive, kind, encouraging, and happy people. Of all the art organizations I have joined, I have always enjoyed being with craftspeople the most. Learning a craft can be done on your own, but private lessons or college classes can be very helpful. A source of income for craftspeople are art fairs and owning a store. It is imperative that the craftsperson know bookkeeping and tax laws if he is to survive running his own business. If your child has a special attraction to working with crafts, encourage him because it makes a very nice hobby to pursue for the rest of his life. An education in art and especially design will add to his enjoyment of his craft because he will then be able to create his own designs. Classes in small business and bookkeeping might also be helpful. Crafts will provide him with a way to relax, a way to create treasured gifts for friends and family, a supplement to his income, friendships, and an area in which he can grow intellectually.

Crafters usually have another source of income, but some have been able to support themselves quite well through art fairs and stores. As our society works a shorter hourly work week, we retire earlier, and we tire of mass production, crafts can be a positive and rewarding way to spend free time. Industry will sometimes hire craftspeople if they have studied in their craft extensively and have an education in industrial design.

JOBS IN ARTS AND CRAFTS

The following list of job titles in visual arts and crafts is taken from the book *Exploring Arts and Crafts Careers,* as published by the U.S. Government Printing Office in 1976.

Commercial Art

ILLUSTRATION

illustrator
general illustrator
technical illustrator
fashion artist
cartographer
cartoonist (printed media)
colorer

medical illustrator
calligrapher
courtroom artist
cartoonist (motion picture,
    television)
scenic artist
architectural renderer

GRAPHIC DESIGN

graphic designer
production manager, advertis-
    ing
director, art
book designer

cover designer
typographer
layout planner
paste-up planner
mechanicals planner

PRINTING PROCESS

printer
compositor
lithographer
etcher
silk screen printer
photoengraver

screen maker, photographic
    process
engraver
music grapher
stripper
color separator

DISPLAYS AND SIGNS

manager, displays
display designer
display artist
director, merchandising display
merchandise displayer

display assembler
sign painter
diorama model maker
sign painter
sign writer, hand

PHOTOGRAPHY

photographer
news photographer
commercial photographer
portrait photographer

I.D. bureau photographer
scientific and biological photo-
    grapher
aerial photographer

finish photographer
candid photographer
photo researcher
photoengraver
photographer, lithographer

photo technician
film developer
photo finisher
photograph retoucher
colorist, photography

Commercial Art: Product Design

INDUSTRIAL DESIGN

industrial designer
commercial designer
model maker
package designer
industrial renderer
patternmaker
sample maker
furniture designer

cabinetry
fixtures
metalwork
musical instruments
jewelry and flatware
glassware
tile
toys

TEXTILE AND FASHION DESIGN

textile designer
cloth designer
screen printer
clothing and accessory designer
copyist

tailor
dressmaker
wallpaper designer
carpet designer

ENVIRONMENTAL DESIGN

architect
architectural drafter
renderer, architectural
architectural modeler
landscape architect

landscape drafter
urban planner
interior designer
stage set designer
miniature set designer

Fine Art

TWO-DIMENSIONAL ART

painter
drafter
muralist

photographer
printmaker
calligrapher

THREE-DIMENSIONAL ART

sculptor

OTHER

experimental materials artist
independent film maker
computer artist

media artist
experimental artist

CRAFTSPERSON

wood
clay
leather
stone
plastic
horn/bone/shell

fiber
glass
metals
print
miscellaneous combined materials

Crafts

HAND CRAFTS/CRAFTSPERSONS AND DESIGNERS

wood design
cabinet maker
woodcarver
boatbuilder
wood sculptor
instrument maker
clay design
ceramicist/clay
potter
tile designer/clay
leather design
leather worker
leather seamstress
belt maker
saddle maker
stone design
sculptor/stone
carver/stone
stone worker

plastic design
jewelry/plastic
sculptor/plastic
fiber design
weaver
basket maker
spinner
dyer
needlemaker
quilt maker
fabric printer
macramaist
non-loom fiber
rug maker
custom sewer
glass design
glass blower
glass decorator
stained glass

mosaicist
metal design
silver/goldsmith
jeweler
metal sculptor
blacksmith
enamelist
printmaking
bookbinder/hand
miscellaneous combined materials

small press printer
soft sculptor
crafts/tools designer
doll house furniture
floral designer
candle maker
paper craftsman
decoupage worker
technical services, fine art
picture framer
mat cutter
fine art printer

Art Education

TEACHING

faculty member, college or university
teacher, secondary school
teacher, elementary school
teacher, kindergarten
teacher, nursery
teacher, visiting

instructor, vocational training
director, art department
teacher, adult education
director, vocational training
art supervisor
educational specialist
instructor, on-the-job training

The above teachers can work in: preschools, private schools, public schools, elementary, junior or senior high schools, specialized schools, community centers, junior colleges, colleges, universities, trade schools, army bases, recreational departments, educational television stations, prisons, private studios, workshops, and retirement homes.

MUSEUM EDUCATION

museum educator
museum designer
publications specialist

publicity specialist
conservator

WRITERS ABOUT ART

critic
art reporter

art reviewer

ART LIBRARIAN

ART THERAPY

art therapist
occupational therapist

expressive or play therapist

Arts Business and Management

ARTS, CRAFTS MANAGEMENT

arts manager
director, art/craft organizations, governmental or private

researcher, art/craft organizations, governmental or private
public relations worker, art/craft organizations, governmental or private

EXHIBITING, SALES, PROMOTION

gallery director
gallery assistant
private dealer
collections "advisor"
director/crafts center
director/crafts fair
craftsperson's agent
artist's agent
publicist

appraiser
cataloguer
owner, retail shop or gallery
manager, photogallery/studio
salesperson, art/craft
director, hobby shop
sales, import crafts
arts/crafts supply salesperson
designer, shop or gallery exhibits

Success in any career, especially the arts, depends upon commitment. If you want your child to be successful in his chosen career, guide him by encouraging his commitment to various projects and organizations that he feels are important. As he learns how to commit to and pursue goals, this will ultimately help him in his career. My two sons were completely committed to football, wrestling, and track during their respective seasons. As the season progressed, their classwork improved, they were delightfully pleasant and helpful around the house, and they "walked tall," showing the world they were very proud, content, and happy. I also find myself happiest when I am working on something I like to do (like writing this book). Once a project is begun, encourage your child to finish it. That commitment will give him a goal that he can pursue with great passion and dedication. The importance of this word—commitment —was made clear when I remembered what my art teacher in high school once told me. "I love your painting, Donna. The colors you chose give it such a peaceful feeling. You have been working on it since early last week and now it's finished. I though you were going to quit, but you never gave up on the pursuit of your goal and we now have a picture that is good enough to hang in the art fair." My teacher then gave me a handshake that I will never forget. Praise your son's or daughter's commitment and you will encourage it.

COMMITMENT

Commitment can be used as a determining factor in career se-lection. If your child finds that he is unable to dedicate himself to-tally to a subject, an organization, or a team, he may be better off joining one with which he can totally commit himself. When I was in high school I joined the band. I liked music, could read notes, and played the clarinet fairly well, but was never truly committed to the band. I liked my teacher and the kids in the band, but I was never dedicated to making the band the very best it could be. As I look back, I probably should not have stayed in it for four years. What if I had joined an organization like the school newspaper? Perhaps it wouldn't have taken forty-six years to discover that I truly loved writing. If I were committed to the newspaper, wouldn't I have ben-efited the school more that I did as a half-committed band mem-ber? Notice the attitude and level of commitment in all that your child does and encourage him to "reroute" it if necessary. Time spent in an organization or an art medium where he is unable to dedicate himself may be time wasted. Every time your child makes a commitment and follows through with it, he will be better able to fulfill his ultimate dream, whether it be a career in art or just a hobby. Commitment will build his self-esteem and direct him in his ultimate career goal: success.

The jobs listed above all require people who have education, training, and/or an interest in the arts. Once your child has chosen a career, he needs to get training and experience. There is a lot of competition for art jobs, but do not let that discourage him. If he is dedicated to his career and is willing to work hard at perfecting his skills, he will eventually be successful.

As his parents, you can help him the most by providing opportunities to develop his art skills before he enters the job market. This can be in the form of a college education, helping him get a job that will train him as he works, art classes that will bring his art skills up to a professional level, financial support while he develops his art form to the point where he can sell it, and/or making sure he has the information he needs through books and professional magazines as he goes through the "lean" years before he gets his first real job.

Upon first entering the job market, he may have to settle for an entry-level job that is only remotely related to his training. For example, if he has trained to be a fabric designer but cannot find this type of work, he may want to take a job cutting patterns or running errands for a textile company. Working in an area related to his skills will enhance his future opportunities, especially if he makes known to his boss and fellow workers that he is ready, willing, and able to help whenever needed and is dedicated 100% to the success of the company.

Several years ago, I met a man who was in my art class back in the '60s. He told me an interesting story about the development of his career. When he first graduated from art school, he wanted to work in a museum's graphic design department promoting the museum. However, there were no openings so he took a job as a museum guard. Several months later the museum's graphic designer was overwhelmed with work and needed help immediately, so he asked my friend's boss if he could be relieved of his duties and help in the graphics department. This was just the beginning of a long and fruitful career working for this art museum. As he approached his forties, he found a new interest in museum management and eventually became the museum's director. When accepting a first job, help your child understand that it is okay to take a position beneath his level of training as long as it is related in some way to his chosen career.

CHOOSING A CAREER

Your child may need help in choosing a career that is best suited to him. You can help him decide by taking into account all available information: the results of his high school vocational interest test, what you know about your child, his own career interests, and suggestions from friends and relatives. If he still does not know what career path to take, you might discuss activities in school that he particularly enjoyed, such as a current events class, being a cheer-leader, learning how to do watercolor or a particular craft, organiz-ing the school's yearbook, or being on the football team. You'll also need to talk about his personality traits: does he like to work by him-self, is he organized, does he enjoy working at a desk or does he need to be active, is making a lot of money important? Be sure to discuss the activities that he *didn't* enjoy. Once you and your child have de-cided on several possible careers, your local reference librarian can search for information about each job. Choosing a career that is right for your son or daughter is difficult but very important.

Some children choose a career very early in life; others need guidance and more time. From the day my son Mark turned ten years old, he knew he wanted to work with machinery and be in the military, so he joined the Navy. My other son has tried several ca-reers and still is not sure what he wants to do for the rest of his life. As you can tell from the list of jobs available for artistic people, there are many choices available, perhaps too many. A decision, however, has to be made and once your child is ready to make it, he needs to make a commitment to dedicate himself totally to learning the skills necessary to be a success in this career. He should not, however, feel that this will be his only career. Many of us will have three or four careers during our working years.

6.

SETTING UP THE WORK AREA

It is very important for your child to have her own area for creating art. It should be special place where she is not afraid to make mistakes, where she can be alone, and where she has access to her favorite art materials. This chapter will tell you how to make an art studio and how to furnish the area so your child can best develop her creativity and artistic talent.

Find a place to set up an art corner. Maybe there is an empty bedroom, a laundry room, a corner of your child's bedroom, or even a space at the end of your hallway that could be used for your child's art studio. Unless your basement is particularly cheery and very dry, I do not recommend it. An attic is preferable to the basement. In fact, if I had my preference, my art studio would be in the attic because it is so secluded and quiet. If your space is extremely limited, you can simply use a bookshelf or cabinet anywhere in the house.

To give up a part of your home so your child can work on art is a generous and loving act that will encourage and increase her desire to do art. This chapter will give you suggestions for setting up and furnishing your child's area for working on art.

FURNITURE FOR THE ART CORNER

In setting up your child's art studio, you will need several pieces of furniture. The most important are work tables. She will need two kinds: one that is flat and, if at all possible, one that slants. Professional artists and draftsmen use a *slanted drawing table* (approximately 30° angle). By providing this type of surface, your child will have less neck and back discomfort, and her drawing will improve because she will be looking at her work at a more natural angle. Artists young and old spend many hours working on their projects and need to be comfortable, so please try to provide this slanted work surface. My work area has a table that can be laid flat or raised up. You can purchase a drawing table, make one out of an old desk, build one, or simply lean a large (18" x 30") board against a stack of books.

Another kind of table your child will need is a *long, flat table*. Here's how we found ours. After a church dinner, my boys and I noticed that one of the tables was in very poor condition. It was a heavy, solid table, but the years had taken their toll on the top. I mentioned this to the minister and told him about my idea for an art area at home. He said, "I would be delighted to let you have it since we just received ten new ones." I covered the top with floor tile adhesive and a piece of heavy countertop vinyl. So for a modest donation we had a table that has served us well for many years. A flat table is necessary for projects like gluing, watercolor or finger painting, sculpture, and crafts. Not only do you have a large surface to work on, but you can store your art supplies underneath. The height of the table will determine whether it can be used in a sitting or standing position. Just as you have high countertops in your kitchen so you can stand and work, your child will enjoy a tall table so she can stand and work once in a while. Some artists use a tall stool at the work table so it can be used in both standing and sitting positions. If your table is too low to be used in a standing position, you can prop up the legs with pieces of wood or cement blocks. A long, flat table is a very important part of your child's art corner.

Another piece of furniture your child will need is a *chair*. This can be a simple stool or it can be a chair with casters (my favorite). If your chair is too high, be sure it has rungs so she can rest her feet or provide a box or foot stool to rest her feet on. If at all possible, try to have the table and chair at the right height. The desk needs to be as high as the top of her legs; the work table for standing up needs to be at hip level; and the chair to the bend in her knees.

A *mirror* should also be placed in the art corner. Many times I will look at my own work and see that it looks good but ... when I look at it in front of a mirror I will usually find the error quickly. A mirror somehow distances the artist from the work and therefore lets her see it with more accuracy.

A desk that slants, a work table, a chair, and a mirror are the main pieces of furniture you will need for your child's art corner.

FLOOR AND WALL PROTECTION

Now you need to have the floors and walls covered. Hardware stores have rolls of *mailing paper,* a brown, medium-weight paper that makes an excellent, inexpensive covering for your walls. You maybe tempted to use white paper but don't—it has too much glare. What's especially nice about mailing paper is that your child can draw, write, and tape her favorite pictures on it, without the fear of ruining the walls. If you are worried the kind of markers or paint your child might use will seep through the mailing paper, you can put a thin layer of plastic on the wall first. Hardware stores sell large sheets of plastic that are used as drop cloths when painting. Look for the kind that is 1 or 2 mil in thickness. Secure the thin plastic sheets to the wall using tape or staples, then hang the brown mailing paper over it. When the paper gets too messy, simply take it down and put up new paper.

The floor also needs to be covered. Even if the floor is not carpeted, I suggest you cover it. This can be done with a heavy plastic (4 mil) sheet, a tarp (a reinforced plastic sheet), a canvas drop cloth (a bit more expensive, but it will last longer and liquids will absorb into it and not puddle as they will on plastic), a sheet of vinyl flooring, or a piece of heavy cloth vinyl. When the inevitable spill happens, your child will not have to worry because the floor will be well protected. You might want to make it clear that when a spill occurs, it needs to wiped up quickly, because it will get onto shoes and travel to less protected areas. To keep the plastic floor covering flat, use duct tape or heavy-duty tape along the edges and down the center. Be sure the plastic extends at least 3 feet beyond the work tables.

Covering the walls and floors will eliminate worry and stress for both you and your child. Art can be a messy business, but with protection, your child's art activities will not harm your walls and floors.

OTHER ITEMS TO PLACE IN YOUR CHILD'S ART CORNER

Your child's art corner needs good *lighting*. Lighting is best when it comes from behind and above the work table. This could be in the form of a ceiling light or a pole lamp. She will also need a desk lamp to keep from straining to see detail. The portable, adjustable swing-arm lamps are nice, but care must be taken so the lamp does not fall over onto the work surface and cause a fire. I prefer regular incandescent lighting, but fluorescent is okay too. If at all possible, situate your child's art corner near a north window. Many artists prefer northern light because it creates less glare.

Art involves using a large variety of materials. To keep your child's work area organized and clean, provide plenty of places to store supplies and cleanup tools. Storage can be easily handled by using shelves, bookcases, plastic crates, and even cardboard boxes.

Your child will be making mistakes, so provide a waste basket, a whisk broom and dustpan, a rag, paper towels, and a bucket of water with a sponge to keep the studio clean. Some other items that will help to keep the art corner organized are large envelopes, file folders, blank photograph albums, scrapbooks, various sizes of plastic trays, small cans with plastic lids, and pencil holders. You might even put a rechargeable electric broom and a container of disposable wet towelettes in the art area. *Pegboard* works well for storing the tools used frequently, such as scissors, tape, and rulers. Another idea is a shoe tray. Whenever my son came into his art area, he took off his outside shoes and put on special slippers. This worked out very well because it not only kept my rugs clean, it helped my son shift mentally into his creative side.

If the work area is organized, your child will be able to work easily. If the work area is cluttered, she may eventually become discouraged. Organization comes naturally for some, others need to be shown how it is done, but most of us just need the proper equipment.

Keep the art furnishings plain—printed wallpaper, white walls, and bright colors are distracting. Keep colors in the light browns or grays. As your child works with the materials, strong colors and disturbing patterns will be a visual interference. Any decorating in the child's art corner needs to be simple and quiet.

If you are fortunate enough to have two children who are interested in art, you may want to have two separate work areas. If you are even more fortunate and have two children who get along and share well, they can share the same art corner; just add an extra chair.

FREE ART SUPPLIES FOR YOUR CHILD

Now that you have everything in place, it's time to start collecting creative art materials. In Chapter 8, I will discuss purchasing art supplies. Here I would like to tell you where you can get "free" art supplies for your child's art studio.

Magazines are a great source of photographs for your child to find pictures of the things she likes to draw or sculpt. Store them all in a box, so she can find them easily. I keep mine in several photo albums and organize them by categories (animals, boats, nature, lettering, people, houses, etc.) for future reference. Clear plastic pages protect the magazine pictures. Be sure to get the kind that do not have a sticky surface so the pictures can be removed easily.

Another art source is *wallpaper books*. Many wallpaper stores will give them away. Kids love the beautiful prints and rarely have trouble thinking of ways to use them.

Scrap paper can be found at quick-print shops. Explain that your child is talented in art and uses a lot of paper, and ask if they would save their misprints and end-of-runs for you. My favorite scrap paper from print shops is the small gummed pads. They make great flicker books (see page 97).

Scraps from sewing like fabric, ribbon, lace, yarn, buttons, and thread can be placed in another container.

Wood scraps from lumber yards are great too, especially for the child interested in sculpture. She can sand, paint, and nail them together. You can ask for them at the lumber yard. Sometimes they have them for sale; most of the time they are free. Blocks of wood provide a lot of fun and are a great way to introduce sculpture.

Your child will probably be collecting *treasures*. For example, she may find a rock that is "beautiful," an old doll, a leaf, an old shoe, or even a stick that looks like a dinosaur. These objects may seem useless or even ugly to you, but they are items that your child chose because they look interesting. As she studies her treasures she

will be learning about looking, not just glancing but looking very closely. Let her fill up a box with special objects. She may even like to put some on shelves or the window sill in her art corner.

Be sure your child has at least *three large storage boxes* to fill with magazines, scrap paper, and treasures. Small containers like shoe or jewelry boxes make good storage for smaller items like buttons, fabric, or yarns. Having supplies readily available will encourage and stimulate creativity.

Now that you've furnished your child's art room, don't be surprised if you are tempted to join in and develop that artistic side of yourself. Many of my friends and some of the world's best artists didn't start their hobbies or careers until later in life. You just need to turn off the "I can't" record and be like your child—open and willing to try almost anything.

Above, you see a portion of a room used as an art studio. It is designed for children of all ages. If your children are quite young you may want to get a lower table to work at and a stand-up painting easel. The total work area is 7' x 9' and can, of course, be modified. If you would like to block off the area from the rest of the room you can use a screen, bookcases, or even a curtain.

EASY-TO-MAKE ART SHELF

For those of you who do not have enough room for an art corner, a book shelf might be the answer (see above). Constantly looking for "this, that, and the other" art supply may be very taxing and may eventually cause your child to lose interest in doing art altogether. Be sure the book shelf is large enough, because it is best to keep all your child's art materials in one central location. My son and I learned the importance of having art supply bookshelves when my son's grandmother gave him an expensive set of drawing pens. Rather than lose them, he decided to put them in a secret place in his room. He told me, "Don't worry, Mom, I won't forget where I put them." Ten years later, we found his pen set safely tucked in between the wood stretchers and the frame of his favorite painting, which incidentally gave us all a good laugh—it was a picture of a large, ferocious lion! My home was very small and I had not provided my son with a bookshelf for his art supplies.

If you are afraid of the book shelf looking unsightly, you can cover the front with a piece of vinyl or cloth. This piece of material can also double as a floor or table protector whenever your child does artwork. Keep the vinyl a plain color, preferably an off-white. Your child will be drawing on this piece of material and will find it difficult to concentrate on her picture if there are bright colors and designs all around her. The fabric can be secured to the shelves with hook-and-loop tape (the rough side secured onto the shelf and the fuzzy side to the vinyl).

You can make a book shelf by using four cement blocks and a long piece of lumber 1" x 15" x 6' (see photo). If you like, paint or cover the cement blocks or use the two center holes as storage areas too. Cement blocks are very heavy, so it will be difficult (not impossible) for your child to pull the shelves over. Whether you decide to make the shelving unit yourself or use one you already have, remember that providing a separate storage area for your child's art materials will keep both of your lives organized and efficient.

IN SUMMARY

A specific place in your home for your child to do her artwork will give her a great deal of encouragement. When you do this, you tell her: I love you, I believe in you, and I am willing to sacrifice part of my living space, because I realize that to succeed in art, you need not only the proper equipment but a special place too.

7.

PROJECTS FOR YOUR CHILD

Perhaps your child has come up to you, at some time or another, and said, "What can I do? I'm bored." In our active lives as parents we find ourselves very busy in our attempt to be teacher, psychologist, referee ... to our child. Being bored sounds a little strange. How can our own children be bored when there is so much to do? It seems the older I get, the less bored I am; in fact, there's usually never enough time to get everything done. But I do remember the days when I was a young girl when time seemed to go on and on. When your artistically inclined child asks you for something to do, you might try one of the activities listed in this chapter. The projects are listed in age groups and designed specifically to develop art skills. Do not limit your child to one age group. He may enjoy doing art projects in the next level above or below him.

Each list of projects is preceded by a few paragraphs describing some of the common characteristics of a child of that age.

PROJECTS FOR CHILDREN AGES 2 TO 5

Studies of young children's first drawings show us that a child will begin drawing by scribbling. You probably remember seeing your two- and three-year-old child take a crayon and make swirls and zigzags all over the paper. My first child, Mark, was so good at this, I had to put a newspaper under his pictures to protect our table.

Scribbling continues for a long time. Right around two and a half years, your child will find a form in his scribbling that he likes. He will be so excited he'll give it a name like "Mom." Of course this isn't the least bit flattering, but we moms develop broad shoulders even before birth. After you have persuaded him that it looks exactly like Dad, give him lots of time and paper to draw his new symbol. He'll probably draw it until you think you can't stand it anymore.

Around age three, your child will discover he can make another symbol. He may call it a dog or a tree. This is his first step in expanding his drawing vocabulary. Some of the first objects a child will draw are a house, a flower, a car, a truck, an animal, a door, and people. Most of his drawings are about his home and family life. As he discovers that he can create these new symbols over and over, he will want to draw them for quite some time. Repeating his drawing symbols makes him feel content and happy. You might think of it this way. Remember the rhymes you enjoyed repeating over and over—ones that are in your memory forever like, "Jack and Jill went up the hill ..." or a favorite high school cheer, "Sway to the left, sway to the right, stand up, sit down, fight, fight, fight." Because we repeated them so often, they are in our memory forever. It feels so good to remember them with such total accuracy that we can't help but break into a big smile. Your child's drawings are that way too. He has finally gotten himself to the point where he can draw a picture that his family recognizes, and it feels so good he wants to draw it again and again. We adults do the same thing only we call it a "doodle." My husband drew a dog with sunglasses in seventh grade that everyone thought was "cool" and he's been drawing (doodling) it ever since. Mine was a man with just his eyes and nose peering over a book page and, of course, a few curly hairs on his bald head and sometimes even a bow on that one tassel of hair. So be patient with your little one. If he's as talented as you think he is and you give him plenty of paper and crayons, he will soon find he needs more symbols to communicate the many ideas inside his head.

At about the age of four or five he will begin changing his symbols. For example, he might change his symbol for an animal into an elephant by adding a long nose, or into a giraffe by adding a long neck. When you see him begin to do this, encourage him to develop his symbol further. You might say to him, "Yes, a giraffe has a very long neck, but what else do you notice (remember) about him? What about his fur, what colors are in it?" As your child reaches five, he will become more adept at recreating what he sees. As his parent, your job is to provide the paper, coloring materials, pencils, and encouragement. Your child will supply the rest.

Below is a list of art projects your preschooler may enjoy.

Coloring Books

Children love coloring books. Some artists feel that they should not be given to children. In fact, I felt that way when I had my children. However, now that I am a grandmother and have had more than a few years of child rearing and teaching, I have taken a closer look at coloring books. If children want them, they must be meeting a need and they cannot be all bad.

Let's look at the good points of coloring books. First of all, your child will develop muscle control. In order for the coloring page to look good, he has to stay inside the lines of the drawing. Second, he learns that art is communication. Each page in the coloring book has a specific message. Third, he learns to vary his coloring technique. He will get tired of coloring all his objects the same way and begin to try new things like using very dark or very light colors.

The "down side" of coloring books is that they are overused. Be careful not to use them to the exclusion of other drawing activities. Your child needs blank paper much more than he needs coloring books. He wants to draw his own pictures because he has lots of ideas in his head that he cannot express in words. If coloring books are used too much, he may also feel inadequate with his own drawings. Their drawings are much better than he could ever create.

A middle-of-the-road approach to the coloring book controversy is probably the best idea. Let your child have coloring books, but always be sure he has a lot of blank paper to make his own pictures. To encourage his ability to draw and create, show more excitement and praise for the drawings he has drawn himself than the ones he has merely colored in.

Mural

Roll out a long sheet of shelf paper onto the floor and let your child and his friends draw on it. Some children may want to draw separate pictures on the mural paper, while others may enjoy working together on one big picture. To encourage them to work together on a large drawing, start them off by putting in a horizon line and some hills. Show them how to use the side of the crayons to cover large areas like the sky quickly. Group murals are an interesting art project because you can have more than one artist. You'll enjoy watching your child as he functions in a group.

Crayons, pencils, and paints aren't the only art materials you can use. Let your child try combining materials on his mural. He can use colored paper, magazine pictures, fabric, and even wallpaper. Hang the mural in the hall, in your kid's room, or if it's a holiday picture, you can put it in the window or on the front door. If you would like to let the children work on it some more, you could hang it up on a well-protected wall area where they could add things to it from time to time. One year I did this with a class of first graders. We made a mural of fish in the ocean. I put a protective layer of brown wrapping paper on a door, then taped our mural paper over it. As the children had free time they would add the fish. You might add to the mural yourself. This is a good chance for everyone in the family to create a picture.

Mural themes that young children enjoy working on include: fish in the sea, houses on a hill, flowers, cars going down a road, dinosaurs or animals in a field, full-length self portrait (you trace around the children's bodies as they lie on the paper, they then fill in the clothes, etc.), alphabet or numbers, snowman scene, and what happens on a rainy day.

Many kids just like drawing on a large sheet of paper. They have no desire to make one big picture. My neighbor lets her grandchildren make this kind of mural. When they come over to her house, she rolls out a large sheet of mailing paper on the floor and lets each of them draw on it while she visits with their parents. Each child draws what he wants anywhere on the paper then signs his name below it. When they get tired of drawing on it, she rolls it up and places it in the cabinet until their next visit. They're always excited to see their mural again and show her all the new things they learned to draw.

Homemade Building Blocks

Building blocks have long been a favorite of young children. You can make them yourself using empty cardboard boxes. First, collect boxes in as many different sizes as possible. To help them retain their shape, stuff the boxes with crumpled newspaper and cover them with vinyl-coated wallpaper. They will last a long time if you secure all the corners with heavy tape. Let your child help you stuff, wrap, and tape them, and he will take better care of his new building blocks.

Your child may want a roof on his building. A large sheet of cardboard or a blanket makes a good roof.

Try to provide as many different sizes of boxes as possible. You might even use the ones that hold food and soaps. The variety will make his constructions more exciting and more challenging. Some interesting boxes he can use in his construction projects are vanilla, detergent, pancake flour, and cake mix boxes. Your local drug store also has a wide variety of small sturdy boxes from their shipments of medicines and cosmetics that would be perfect for making building boxes. Cover and tape them so they will all look uniform.

If you have no place to store the building blocks, they can be put under the bed in a large, low cardboard box, placed in a large net and suspended from the ceiling, or stacked one on top of the other in a corner of the room. To keep the boxes from falling over, tie a long heavy cord from the ceiling to the floor with an eye hook at each end. The cord will hold the boxes in the corner until he is ready to use them again.

Creative Blobs

This is an all-time favorite art activity for both kids and adults. Fold a piece of paper in half, then open it up. Put several large drops of paint near the center fold. Fold it in half again and rub your hand over the paper. The large drops of paint inside will be moving around creating an identical design on both halves of the paper. When your child opens his folded paper, his eyes will light up, a big smile will beam across his face, and he may even want to identify it.

Encourage him to add things with his crayon, such as antennae, eyes, hair, or feet. You can also try using more than one color of paint. Make about ten of these together, let them dry, and then send your child off on his own to finish them. Be sure to hang up at least one or two of his favorites. Be prepared to do it again; this is one art activity kids of all ages enjoy.

Gluing Magazine Pictures

Young children usually use too much glue. They are absolutely certain that if they use a lot of glue it will stick better. This project will show them, beyond a shadow of a doubt, that a lot of glue is not a good idea.

For this project your child will need a little help from you. Get out your old magazines and let your child look for pictures of things he enjoys. My granddaughters like picture of dolls, while my grandson likes pictures of food and puppies. Cut them out and let your child glue the pictures onto sheets of colored construction paper. Let him glue them the way he wants to even if it is too much glue. Point out that when he uses too much glue, the picture are all wavy; sometimes even torn or folded in places. Have him try again, until he sees for himself that when you glue paper, it is best only to use a small amount. I tell my young art students, "When you are gluing paper, less is better. Having more crayons may be better than just a few, but just a little glue works better than a lot." Once he understands how to use glue, you can cut a stack of pictures and let him work on his own.

Understanding Colors

Adults are so familiar with colors and their names that we find it hard to understand why our young children are not able to match the words to the colors. However, if you look closely at each color, you will notice many variations. For example, take the color blue—you will rarely see it in its purest form. It may be full of green, making it turquoise, or it may have a little red in it, making it violet. Your child has to decide whether it is blue or green, blue or purple. This takes a lot of practice.

Here's an idea that will be fun for your child and help him learn colors. Together, collect color photographs from magazines. Help your child cut out individual colors or just let him tear them out. For example, in a picture of a little girl in gray pants and a red sweater, you would only cut out the red sweater. Organize the colors in envelopes labeled as to the color he is to put inside. To help him, crayon the color on the envelope along with writing the word. Help him get started by putting approximately three colored pictures in each envelope. For now, only use the basic colors like red, yellow, blue, green, orange, and purple. If there is a question as to where a color should go, hold the picture up to each envelope and see if your child knows which one it looks like the most. If your child truly doesn't know, he is probably not ready for this activity, so wait three or four months and try again. Color discrimination in children can begin as early as two or as late as five years of age. If he continues not to understand color differences after age five, consult your pediatrician or eye doctor.

Drawing and Coloring

I strongly advise you to provide your child with a lot of blank paper. Buy it by the ream and you'll save a lot of money. It's important for your child to release his emotions and thoughts onto paper.

To get him in the mood, let him draw swirls, zigzags, straight lines, and curves—just let him scribble. It's a lot of fun; you might even enjoy doing it with him. As he scribbles, he will begin to release some of his energy and frustrations. I use scribbling as a drawing warmup exercise with all my students. Before you throw the drawings away, just for fun, take his scribble pictures and add in little cars, people, animals, or even facial features—eyes, ears, nose, and mouth. Afterward, he will be relaxed and ready to settle down into serious drawing. Allowing your child to draw will give him a great deal of satisfaction that he cannot get watching television, entertaining his friends, and playing with toys.

Seed Designs

In this project, you and your child will create a picture using seeds and dried beans. The first thing you will need is a piece of cardboard, as paper will be too flimsy. Collect seeds that are colorful and different sizes and shapes. If you can find one very large seed, it will help his design by giving it a *focal point* (a center of interest, a place for your eye to rest as you are looking at the design). Some seeds you might use are bird seed, sunflower seeds, dried lima beans, split peas, red kidney beans, etc. A large seed could be a peach pit or half a walnut shell. Place each kind of seed in a separate container. Before you begin, you can do one of three things. You can practice laying out all the seeds until you see a design you like; you can draw a design on the cardboard to show where to put the seeds; or you can just start gluing down seeds in one area and let the picture unfold. The glue can either be placed directly on the cardboard and seeds set into it, or the glue can be spread over a small area. Your child may enjoy using a small pair of old tweezers to pick up each seed. Keep the cardboard very small if you want him to finish the picture in one sitting. To hang it up, you can tie a string through two holes at the top. Seed pictures look especially nice in the kitchen.

Easy to Make Salt Clay

Children love to create sculptures. Salt clay can provide an inexpensive and easy alternative to the more expensive and difficult sculpture materials.

Mix 2 cups flour and 1 cup salt. Add 1 cup water a little at a time until the consistency seems right. Knead for approximately ten minutes. It is now ready to use. Your child can flatten it, cut out shapes, make long squiggly worms, or roll it into balls. These in turn can be made into animals, alphabet letters, smiley faces, etc. To put two pieces together, just moisten the two areas to be joined and press together until secure. When your shape is done, let it air-dry for forty-eight hours. The unused dough can be stored in a plastic bag in the refrigerator for up to five days. For color, add food coloring to the dough or paint it after it has dried. To keep the dried salt clay sculpture from absorbing water and becoming soft again, cover it with an acrylic varnish on the front and back.

Cutting Squares

Young children love using their scissors, but doing so with any degree of accuracy takes a great deal of skill. Hold a pair of scissors in your hand and watch your hands as you cut something. Your thumb pushes while your first finger pulls, and then your second finger helps your first finger and your ring finger and little finger "hold on for dear life." Cutting with scissors is a big challenge for a small child. But kids love it, so be patient as they struggle. If you give them ample opportunity to use their scissors, it won't take long for them to master the skill of cutting.

Some parents are afraid their children will get cut or fall on the scissors and will not allow them to use scissors. Because of many children's lack of practice, it can take as long as five years to learn how to cut well. Provide your child with rules about where he can and cannot cut and take the scissors away the first time he disobeys.

Be sure to return them in a few minutes, so he can have another chance to do it right. Punishment of a child this young must be kept short to be effective.

In this project your child will be cutting strips of paper into squares and then gluing them onto a surface to create a design. He can use any kind of paper you can find: magazines, newspaper, colored construction paper, paper bags, tissues, or just one kind of paper. Have your child cut these papers into strips, then have him cut the strips into small squares.

Glue the squares onto a piece of paper, a juice can, or a piece of cardboard. Be sure to remind your child to use just a small amount of glue on each square of paper. He can lay them side by side, overlap the pieces, or even have spaces between them. When he is all done you can hang up his work, or if you want to protect it, you can brush on acrylic varnish or cover with clear plastic laminate.

Easel Drawing

If you don't have an easel or a drawing table, you can let your child draw on the refrigerator or on a protected wall. If you need to protect the drawing surface, put a piece of brown mailing paper over it. When his crayon slips, he will not be concerned because it will be on the brown paper. After he is done drawing, roll the drawing up for another day. If he can't think of anything to draw, here are a few suggestions:

- a big, bright sun
- a house with grandpa waving out the window
- you sleeping in your bed
- the stars at night
- how you felt when you were (a sad time) _____
- how you felt when we went (a happy time) _____
- your feet—how many toes do you have on each foot?
- your hands—how many fingers do you have?
- it's raining and you forgot your umbrella
- a big, long, red truck is being unloaded; what is inside?
- everyone in our family
- you and your dad/mom _____ (fishing, swimming, playing ball ...)
- one big tree and lots of little ones
- flags

- flowers—make them all sizes, colors, and shapes
- a boat with someone skiing behind it
- a cat watching television
- the clock on the wall

The important thing in giving a drawing suggestion to your young child is that it be open-ended; an idea that will get him started. If he finishes too quickly, you can usually get him to work on it longer by praising his efforts. Choose one or two things you like about it and see if he forgot something. An example is that when my students drew flowers, more often than not, they forgot the leaves. Almost every flower has leaves. If you mention it in a humorous, non-critical way, he will probably change it. Your child will enjoy drawing on a vertical plane. It gives him more freedom by allowing him to stand up and move around as he works and, much more important, a better view of the picture as he works on it. The best drawing surface is vertical with the bottom slightly slanted toward the artist.

You obviously will not be able to hang up all your child's artwork in your home, but displaying his work is an important sign of support, so here are a few suggestions. Line up four or five drawings and take a vote on which ones to keep. He might want to send a few to grandpa, store some away, or let you take some to the office. Ask your child if it is okay to throw the rest away. It is important for him to realize that not all his work is good enough to keep. If he doesn't want them thrown away, they can be stored in a big envelope or box in his room.

Painting

All children love to paint, but unfortunately, it does make a great deal of mess. There are actually only a few hints that I can give you to help you if you want to allow your child to paint. Purchase an easel or let him work at your table. Be sure he has large-handled brushes, at least five water cans to clean the paint off the brushes, a small sponge or two for accidental spills, large 12" x 18" paper, large cakes of tempera paint, and a lot of newspaper or plastic to protect your table and floor. At this age, more mess may be made if the child cleans up, so I suggest you do all the cleanup. Let him spend his energy painting, and you stand guard until he is done. If you are very lucky and have a child who can clean up and who is very careful with paints, you can and probably should allow him to paint as often as he wishes. Painting is one of the most exciting media in art.

Paper Fastener Creations

Children love paper fasteners. You remember, the ones you used to secure the hands on the clocks made in first and second grade. Your child can make people with arms that wave, kittens with tails that wag, and even a swing that moves back and forth.

Postcards to Friends and Relatives

Children are given so much by friends and relatives that they sometimes forget to say thank you. A postcard is an inexpensive and easy way to encourage your child's practice of good manners. You can help him by writing the words on the back, but let him design the front. Keep plenty of postcards on hand, because grandma is really going to love getting mail from her grandchild. Postcards can also be used as invitations, get-well cards, and I-love-you notes. A young friend of mine sent her dad a card where he worked. Needless to say, he was very surprised and delighted when he got his mail that day. We all love to get a card in the mail, especially one that someone has taken the time to create just for us.

Tracing Around Objects

In this project, your child will make a picture by drawing around objects found in the kitchen. First, have your child sit on a smooth, hard area of the floor with a piece of paper, crayons, and a bowl. Have him trace around the bottom of the bowl onto the paper. It may not be a perfect circle, but accuracy is not necessary for this kind of picture. Now gather up about ten other items in your kitchen that he can trace around. You might use cans, boxes, wooden spoons, plastic cups, and measuring cups. Encourage him to use different colors, to draw over the entire page, and to overlap the shapes. The picture he has just created will look like an abstract line drawing.

He can take this modern abstract drawing one step further by selecting and removing one small section of his drawing. Professional artists will sometimes use this method when they aren't happy with the layout of a picture. Take a piece of lightweight cardboard approximately 9" x 12" and cut a hole in the middle, the size and shape of an index or postal card. The cardboard with the hole in it will be his view finder. Let your child move the cardboard across the drawing until he finds a particularly interesting section of the picture through the opening. This is the part of the picture you are going to save. Trace around the rectangle and then cut out this small section of his drawing. It will look almost like an abstract painting. He can then mount it on an index card or glue it to a postal card. He can also use the view finder on his other paintings.

PROJECTS FOR CHILDREN AGES 6 AND 7

At ages six and seven your child will want to work at perfecting all her new art skills. Until now, she didn't have enough control of the muscles in her hands to give good results. Now that she's a little older, she can cut with more accuracy, color neatly, glue without making a mess, and draw almost anything she can see or imagine.

Being six and seven is an exciting time for a child because she can now draw just about anything that comes to mind. Six and seven year olds will attempt to draw things I wouldn't even begin to consider. For example, a first grade student of mine saw the Golden Gate Bridge on a trip to California. He explained to me that this was what he wanted to draw and before I had a chance to ask him if he was sure, he had drawn the entire bridge. What a great age! I wish that pioneer spirit were still in me so I would be less apprehensive about starting grand art projects.

Children at this age need to be encouraged to work on each of their pictures for at least fifteen minutes. In my art classes there were always a few students who would finish their drawing assignment in an astonishing two or three minutes and appear at my desk saying, "I'm done!" If your child does this, encourage her to spend more time on her picture by talking about it with her. For example, you might say, "I like the way you drew grandma's hair, but isn't there something very important about her face that you forgot?" or "Your house looks so tall and colorful. I wonder who lives inside." When you talk to your child about the items in the picture, your child will realize their importance and will be encouraged to develop them further.

Another way to encourage her to work longer on a picture is to tell her to use the whole piece of paper. If you see she is drawing only on one section of her paper, help her understand that she needs to use the whole paper. This concept will become clear if you show her how other artists use all their surface area to communicate their message. Point out that famous paintings, advertisements in magazines, and business signs use the top, bottom, left, right, and middle of the entire picture. If there is an area left empty, it is usually for a reason.

Your child will also work on her picture longer if she adds detail. When she draws a house, remind her to put in the shutters, the windowsills, the brick, door knobs, shrubbery, flowers, trees, walks, driveways, etc. Detail adds interest to a picture.

By encouraging her to expand on what she has already drawn and to use the entire piece of paper, you will find that she will work on her pictures well over fifteen minutes. By age seven or eight, she might even work on the same picture for more than an hour.

Your child at this age will try just about any new art material you set before her. Some of the art materials you might let her try are chalk, white charcoal pencils, origami, stitching with yarn, weaving, cutting paper, and clay. You might even keep a special box of found items like Popsicle sticks, funny-shaped rocks, pine cones, tree branches, string, empty tape spools, parts from broken toys, etc. Let her experiment with art supplies and found objects. She will enjoy the challenge, and as she works with these supplies she will be developing her creativity.

This is an age at which your child will give you a lot of presents, often in the form of artwork. You have probably wondered just what to do with all of them. I have found it is best just to thank her, enjoy the pictures for a while, and then throw the artwork away. If she says anything, tell her you truly enjoyed it, but if you kept them all, there would be no room for you to display her new projects. Save at least one or two projects a year so you both can enjoy them when she's older. Another way to handle too much artwork is to vote on several pieces that she has completed. Line them up and let her vote on the one to save. The rest of the pictures can be thrown away or kept in a box in her room. The concept of not saving all my artwork became very clear when I was learning how to make pottery in college. My teacher said to the class, "If you keep every single piece of pottery you make in my class and it will take you approximately two years to perfect your skills, you will have saved 800 pots and only ten or twenty of them would be well-made." Your child is just learning how to create art and although some of her work is good, some of it is just part of the learning process and should be treated that way.

This is a great age for kids. They can finally do artwork with enough skill to do it all by themselves; they have the coordination to work without creating a big mess; and they now realize that if they make a mistake, it's no big deal because they can do it again.

Drawing Live Animals

Encourage your child to draw your pets or the animals she sees outside. If at all possible, let her hold one, so she can feel the texture of its fur or skin. Point out the details like the eyelashes or toenails of the animal. If she cannot hold it, talk about the way it looks and how it might feel. About ten years ago, I had the opportunity to feel a stuffed owl at a nature center. The guide allowed me to touch the soft, delicate breast feathers of a barn owl. I never really understood just how soft they were until I felt them myself. Now, whenever I see a drawing or painting of a barn owl, I look to see if the artist captured this softness in his work.

You may have to point out things about the animal that your child may not see at first. I brought my cat, Tonto, to a drawing class one afternoon and showed him to the boys and girls. We talked about Tonto and the children held him, they told the class what they saw. One of the children said, "Look at his eyes. We have round dark spots in the center of our eyes, but Tonto has an oval dark spot in his eye." Most of the pictures drawn that afternoon had oval eyes, long whiskers, eyelashes, the back legs drawn bigger than the front, with fluffy fur and a jingle bell collar. An interesting way to draw animals is to have your child first draw the animal from memory, then have her draw it again after she has actually seen it and studied it.

Origami

Origami is the art of paper folding. The most familiar origami is the paper sailor's hat and the paper airplane. There is a special fascination a child feels when she sees her parent transform a simple piece of paper into an airplane. She will enjoy trying to make one too. If she really likes origami, get a beginner's level book on paper folding from the library. She can decorate her creations herself using crayons, adding streamers, gluing on foil designs, or writing words on them. Other paper-folding projects she will be able to make are fans, a paper box, and a pop-up spring for a card.

Painting

The paper you use for painting will need to have some body to it. I suggest a 60-80 lb. manila or sulphite paper. This is also an excellent drawing paper. Buy it by the ream (500 sheets). I can almost guarantee none of it will go to waste. The easiest paints to work with, for both you and your child, are tempera cakes. Watercolor is actually a very difficult medium. It requires a lot of skill and special paper, which is very expensive. Save yourself some money and your child a lot of frustration and do not purchase a set of watercolor paints until she is at least thirteen. Tempera paints are inexpensive and come in solid cakes that make them easy to use and clean up. I recommend you purchase good paint brushes and teach her to take care of them. After every use, wash them in warm, soapy water (be sure to remove all the paint, especially at the base of the brush), rinse well, and store with the bristles in a horizontal position. If brushes are stored upright, the water will soften the glue that secures the bristles. Storing them downward will, of course, destroy their shape. She can also paint with foam brushes, sponges, and cotton swabs. Provide several containers of water for rinsing brushes. Paper towels or napkins come in handy. That's basically all you need: paint, paper, paint brushes, something to protect the table or floor, water containers, and some paper towels.

If she can't think of anything to paint, here are a few suggestions you can offer to get her started:

- a flower—put a real flower in front of her and let her paint it. Encourage her to "put it somewhere," for example, in a garden, in a vase, or on someone's dress.
- a snowy winter scene—this kind of picture looks especially good on blue or black construction paper.
- a tree in a specific season
- an animal
- your home
- if you could have one thing right now, what would it be?
- later today, I would like to _____.
- it rained so hard, _____.
- portrait of friend and herself
- fishing from a pier or boat

- underwater
- airplanes or rockets in the sky
- cars going down the highway

You can write these on small pieces of paper and put them in a jar so she can choose one when she is stuck for ideas. She might also want to put some of her own ideas in the jar.

Suggested projects are best if they are open-ended, so your child can add her own thoughts and ideas. You might ask whether her picture answers the standard journalism questions: who, what, when, where, why, and how. Most of my young art students would answer the "when" question by making their paintings "a sunny day." This is actually a reflection of their continual happy dispositions. Encourage your child to notice that not every day is sunny—we have cloudy and rainy days—and she might even paint a picture about what the world looks like at night.

Realistically speaking, painting involves a lot of work on your part. It is an activity that will probably not be repeated very often if there is a continual mess, especially if you have the sole responsibility of cleaning it up. I suggest that you *clearly* show her how the setup and cleanup are to be done, then let her do most of it herself. Be sure to provide the kind of cleanup materials she can easily use. For example, give her a small sponge that will fit in her hand, and provide two buckets only half filled with water, one for clean water and one for dirty water. This will keep her away from your sink. Painting is a wonderful and exciting art activity that most children truly enjoy.

Greeting Cards

There are many beautiful cards on the market, but there is nothing more moving than receiving a handmade card. Now that your child is six or seven, she'll be able to create her own greeting cards.

You can purchase blank greeting cards from an art supply store and let your child put designs on them, or she can make the cards herself. An easy way to make a card is by cutting a piece of paper twice the size of a regular envelope and folding it in half.

Before your child begins working on her card, encourage her to sketch out her design on scrap paper. If she makes several designs, you can help her choose the best one to put on the card. Drawing and coloring are not the only ways to decorate a card. My students have created cards by cutting out pictures from magazines, using pressed flowers, and stitching the paper with embroidery thread. One student made a beautiful card for her grandmother by simply cutting a heart from a scrap of fabric. We also made designs by taking a half of a raw potato and carving a small raised symbol into it and then dipping only the raised part of the potato into paint and pressing it onto the card (a simple form of print making).

Making greeting cards is also a chance for your child to make some money. If her cards are really good, let her set up a card display so family and friends can purchase them. One of my students put his name and the date on the back of his cards and then penciled in the price next to it: "Cards by Ken, one dollar."

Sock Puppets

An old sock can be turned into a puppet by adding eyes, a mouth, and a nose. To make it extra funny, add roll-around eyes. If you glue the eyes right onto the stretchy sock material, they may fall off, so first glue them onto a piece of felt or cloth and then secure it to the sock. Yarn and curled ribbon make good hair. This is a project you will want to do together, at least for the first one. To encourage your child to make more puppets, display them somewhere in the house. My kids liked to put name tags and little poems next to them. Some materials you can use on sock puppets are felt, yarn, ribbon, lace, leather, scrap fabric, old ties, and sequins. To help her learn how to use a puppet, have her bring one with her next time you read a book aloud. She'll enjoy letting her puppet ask questions.

Stringing Beads

Your child can make a necklace, a decoration for the house, or an unusual toy by stringing beads. As she does so, she will develop hand/eye coordination and increase her manual dexterity. When she works with beads, encourage her to repeat colors and styles of beads. For example, she could repeat over and over three red beads, one white, and two pink or repeat three large round beads, two medium round beads, and five small beads. By repeating sets of beads, she will realize that repetition creates rhythm. She will also find that if she uses repetition in all her art projects, they will have a quality that is very satisfying to the eye. Point out to your child that repetition is all around us in our everyday world: in the leaves on a tree, the rocks in a brook, and the windows on a tall building. That is why repetition looks so good in our artwork. It reminds us of the beauty around us.

You can find a wide variety of beads at arts and crafts stores or you might let your child string some dried noodles. Be careful in selecting the correct size needle for stringing the beads. It will have to be small enough to go through the smallest beads put on the string. Some six year olds can thread their own needles, but if yours cannot, let her practice with a needle with as large an eye as possible and then try a needle with a smaller eye until she learns how. Working with beads helps your child develop the muscles in her hands and teaches her the important design principle of repetition.

Sculpture—Strange Creatures

Your child will enjoy making wild and strange creatures out of old discarded objects like Popsicle sticks and feathers. She may even want to create her own dinosaur. Before she begins a sculpture, she will need something to mount it on—a base. The base can be as simple as a piece of cardboard or a plastic lid or as nice as a block of wood. Some items your child could use for this project are wire, feathers, cotton, toothpicks, Popsicle sticks, plastic movable eyes, beads, sequins, buttons, yarn, bottle tops, plastic lids, old pencils, sticks, small rocks, fluorescent paper scraps, ribbon, and fabric scraps.

To glue the pieces together, you can use white glue for the porous materials and a tacky or multi-purpose glue for adhering the metals and plastics. When you purchase glue for young children to use, be sure it is nontoxic and won't adhere to skin. A large square of oilcloth or fabric-backed vinyl will protect your table and not stick to the project.

You might help your child get started on this project by securing the first few pieces to the base. She can do the rest. When she is ready to show it to everyone, the family might suggest names for her creation. Your child may even write a poem about who it is, what it is about to do, when it lived, where it is going, why it is here, and how it came into being. Sculpture takes a lot of imagination and is therefore a lot of fun for children six and seven years old because they are so full of ideas.

PROJECTS FOR CHILDREN AGES 8 AND 9

As your child approaches ages eight and nine, you will probably find all your dreams about being a parent have come true. At least for me, this was *the* best age while raising my two sons. When I taught in public schools, I enjoyed teaching art to third graders more than any other grade. They are usually enthusiastic, energetic, orderly, clean, optimistic, happy, and pleasant children. One of the most endearing qualities about them is that they help you laugh at your mistakes. Here is an example. One afternoon I was drawing on the chalk board and got so carried away with talking *and* drawing, my picture began to lean progressively toward the bottom of the chalk board. At first, I heard a snicker, then the whole class began to laugh. The boat I was drawing was not only sinking, the water was draining out of the ocean. It almost looked as though the boat was going down a drain. I felt very embarrassed; after all, I was their art teacher. Somehow, I managed to laugh along with them, although I'm sure my face was as red as a beet. As the year progressed, I learned from these dear, sweet third graders to laugh at myself. They really didn't care if I made a mistake. They wanted to learn how to draw and as long as they can learn something from me, a mistake here and there was no big deal; they've been doing it for years themselves.

Artistically, the child this age is now ready to do some serious drawing. Of all the various art forms, your child will primarily be interested in learning how to draw. This is a good time to go to the book store or library and get how-to-draw books. Try to find him drawing books about the things he enjoys looking at and reading about in books and magazines. In general, the boys usually want drawing books on cars, trucks, rockets, airplanes, and super heroes. Some girls, however, will choose to draw cars and airplanes, and some boys will enjoy drawing flowers and people. Many drawing books are too difficult for eight- and nine-year-old children. The best ones for this age stress breaking all drawing subjects into a basic circle or square and doing only a small amount of shading. Give your child a lot of paper, a good #2B drawing pencil, an eraser and, if possible, a slanted table, and he will thoroughly enjoy the challenges ahead in his pursuit of learning to draw.

Sculpture is a good activity for the eight and nine year old. He enjoys it but is usually not as successful as he would like to be. Encourage him to try, and applaud his efforts. Keep a box of odds and ends as stated for six and seven year olds, and he will enjoy making wild, crazy creatures. A good sculpture medium for eight or nine year olds is self-hardening modeling clay. Although his main interest will probably be drawing, sculpture will help him improve his drawing because it forces him to think more about proportions.

Cleanup is usually no problem at this age. Enjoy it while you can. Many children lose this endearing quality of wanting to clean up after themselves, and it doesn't return till they are living on their own. This is not to say that all children are messy during their preteen and teenage years; if you have a neat child you are truly blessed.

Rewards at this age are usually not necessary, and your child may even frown upon them. It's better to give him a present than a reward. A present will show him you are happy with his behavior and especially proud of his artwork. You might surprise him with a new drawing pencil, a picture or sculpture of something he likes to draw, or a book.

Drawing with a Border

We all enjoy a picture much more if it is in a frame. We know that we are to look only inside the frame to find the picture, nowhere else. Most of your child's pictures will not be of framing quality for quite some time, but your child can make his picture look like it has a frame by putting a border around his drawing.

Before he begins drawing, have your child mark off a $1/2$" or $3/4$" line with a ruler on each of the four sides of his drawing paper. The easiest way to do this is to make the border the width of the ruler. Line it up with the edge of the paper, but leave a small edge of the paper visible so you can be sure the ruler is perfectly straight, and then draw the line on the other side of the ruler. Be sure he draws his picture first, then designs the border. He may decide just to color it brown to look like wood or he might put a design in it. The decorations in the border might even lend a humorous tone to the picture. Last year one of my students drew a picture of a Guernsey cow and put glass milk bottles in the border. A professional artist friend of mine employs this border idea in all her oil paintings; in fact she never even uses a frame.

Picture Scrapbook

Your child will probably have one subject he loves to draw more than anything else. He more than likely has a photograph of it somewhere in his room and is continually trying to draw it better than he did the last time. If he has several photographs, he will learn a great deal more about drawing it.

This is a great time to start a picture scrapbook of all his favorite subjects. Photo albums with clear plastic over each page work best. Do not get the kind with adhesive pages because he will want to remove his pictures from time to time.

Scrapbooks are nice to have because when your child is not sure how to draw, for example, the wings on his B-52 bomber, he knows where to find a photograph of it and can then quickly get back to his drawing. Relying on memory may not be what he wants to do.

At this age, your child is probably very serious about drawing his subject as best he can. Your whole family can pitch in and help him find pictures for his scrapbook.

Weaving

Children at this age love to weave. The best way to help them understand the concept of weaving is with paper. Perhaps you remember doing this in grade school. You take two different colors of paper and weave them together. Begin by cutting one piece half the size of the other. Fold the big piece in half and make $1/2$" slits starting at the folded edge and cutting to $1/2$" short of the edge of the paper. Take your smaller piece of paper and cut it into $1/2$" strips. Open up your larger paper, and one by one weave strips over and under each slit in the large paper. Many children like to use these as place mats. Unusual designs can be made by cutting the strips wavy, zigzag, angled, thick, and even super-thin. Clear Contact® paper can be used to protect and preserve them.

When he understands this kind of weaving, he can work on a cardboard loom with yarn. You can purchase one from an art catalog or make one out of heavy cardboard. The cardboard should be about 6" x 12" and have $1/4$" notches all across the top edge (6" side) of the cardboard for a total of 24 notches. They should be $1/2$" deep. Cut notches on both 6" sides and be sure the cuts are exactly opposite each other. Wind string continuously around the cardboard, placing each round in a notch both at the top and at the bottom. The notches are there to hold each round of string in place. You can have as few as five rounds or as many as the board will hold. Tie the two ends of the string crosswise in the back. Using a weaving needle or your hands, take a piece of yarn and go over, under, over, under each string until you get to the other side. Take the remaining yarn and go back the other way. Go back and forth until you either use up the yarn or want to use another color. As you complete each row, push it up close to the one above it. If you find the sides of your weaving pulling in, you are pulling too tight as you round the corner for the next row. It is best to begin and end each piece of yarn somewhere in the middle of the row. The best way to end a row of one color is to leave about 2" of yarn hanging; don't cut it off right at the weaving. When your weaving is complete, you can hide these ends inside the weaving by pulling them through the weaving with a small needle. Try not to make any knots; a good weaving has no knots. If this is too confusing, you can find beginning weaving books in the library or you can purchase a cardboard weaving kit with complete instructions from an art supply store. The kits are inexpensive and well worth the money.

A weaving looks best when it has repeated colors. Your child should try to repeat the colors of yarn by using a lot of one color, a small amount of another, and a medium amount of the other colors. This is a basic design principle, used not only with color but shapes and textures, that he can apply in all his artwork.

My students and I made wall hangings, purses, and mug rugs. The cardboard looms were so popular that I had parents and other teachers wanting to learn how to weave on them, so you might want to get one for yourself too. Weaving is a very relaxing art activity.

White Pencil Drawing

Drawing can take on a new excitement when your child uses a white charcoal pencil on dark paper. My students especially enjoyed drawing trees with white pencils, then they would add gravestones, old abandoned buildings and, of course, a ghost or two. Your child might also make a picture of snow-capped mountains, silver jets flying across the moon, a big fluffy white owl sitting in a tree, a bowl of vanilla ice cream, or just lettering. Drawing with white is an interesting challenge for your child because it's the opposite of his usual drawing medium.

Create a New Game

Your child might enjoy making his own game. But before he begins, first have him study all the games he has collected over the years. Talk about the different kinds he has amassed: card games, board games, manual dexterity games, word games, games that use dice or money. Then encourage him to try to think of one on his own.

He should first make a paper model to make sure his idea works. You might let him try it out on you. It will probably take two or three rough drafts before it is ready to be made in its final form. The final project has to be well-made and look good or no one will want to play it. Art materials he can use to make his game are self-hardening clay, buttons, cardboard, paper, plastic cans, photographs, rulers, paint, index cards, colored pencils, and a strong box to store it in.

Your child will put a lot of work into his game. Be sure to play it at least once with him and then encourage him to show it to his friends. Next time he plays a game, he will appreciate not only the time it takes to create a game, but the artwork in the boards, the cards, the playing pieces, and the cover of the box.

Puppets

Your child will enjoy making puppets at this age, perhaps even more than using them. Sock puppets were mentioned in the section for five and six year olds, and eight- and nine-year-old children will enjoy making them too. At this age he will be able to put braids, buttons, long forked tongues, and even hats on his puppets. When your child has made a few, be sure he puts them on display for the rest of the family to enjoy.

Papier maché puppets are easy and fun to make. Small strips of newspaper are dipped into watered-down white glue, then draped over an inflated balloon until there are at least five layers. Have him put a small stem on the balloon for the neck of the puppet. This will give your child a place to secure the cloth shirt and to help him hold the puppet on his finger. When the papier maché is dry and not cool to the touch, deflate the balloon and pull it out. Paint on facial features, glue on hair, and add a circle of cloth for the puppet's shirt.

Encourage your child to use his puppet. He can tell a younger child a story, bring the puppet to the dinner table with a nightly joke for the family, or create a full puppet show. Some children enjoy just making them and leave the performing to others.

Clay Sculpture

Most children love to work with clay, but there are a few who insist that it is just too messy. There are four kinds of clay. One is the traditional clay that requires a kiln to complete the drying process. Another is a non-hardening clay. It can be used over and over and (almost) never hardens. A third kind of clay is self-hardening; you can work with it and let it dry until it becomes hard enough to paint. A fourth kind of clay is one that you place in the oven to make it hard. This is probably the best kind of clay for the eight or nine year old.

Sculpture is actually a very difficult medium, but your child will probably enjoy the challenge. In my art classes we made pottery, animals, rocket ships, cars, monsters, snakes, and people. For clay sculpture, your child will need clay modeling tools, a rotating platform to place his sculpture on as he works, and a piece of fabric-backed vinyl to cover his work area on the table. He will also enjoy a few good books about making sculpture.

PROJECTS FOR CHILDREN AGES 10 AND 11

Parenting becomes a real challenge as your child reaches ten and eleven years old. A common trait of children this age is their sensitivity to criticism. To keep your child working at developing her art skills, give her a lot of praise. Negative comments of any kind may be so discouraging that she may give up artwork. You also need to be watchful of other people in your child's life making negative comments about her artwork. If you notice your child has quit working, you might talk to her about it. Maybe someone has criticized her work because that person was jealous. The person might have said it as a way of helping her, and your child misinterpreted it as a personal attack.

Criticism needs to be about what she has *done*, not about her personally. One of my fifth grade art students had drawn cats since she was in second grade. She thought her drawings were a pretty good representation of her beloved Fluffy until the latter part of fourth grade. She was particularly sensitive at this age and her class-mates sensed it. They began to tease her about her cat drawings. By fifth grade she not only gave up drawing cats but all her other art-work too. Drawing wasn't fun anymore. Perhaps this all could have been avoided if her parents had discussed it when they first noticed she had stopped drawing cats. They might have encouraged her in-terest by purchasing her a cat sculpture or cat calendar, checking out several books about cats, framing one of her old cat pictures, or by getting her a new kitten.

Be careful with your child. Tell her that in order to learn any-thing well, she will be making many mistakes. Tell her all the mis-takes you made when you were learning something. Her artwork will not look very good at first and her friends may tease her, but she must persevere if she really wants to learn how to draw.

The man who makes no mistakes does not usually make anything.
William Connor Magee, 1868

For the first time in her life, she will probably be embarrassed about the quality of her artwork. She will also be very critical of her-self. Your job as parent is to help her understand that this criticism of her work will be the driving force she will need to become a good artist. An artist is rarely content with her work — it's never good enough. There is always one small area where she could have done better. Tell her stories about how many mistakes you made as you learned to cook, drive a car, or wash clothes. Always remember that she will be critical enough of her own work; she doesn't need you to be critical too. She needs you to be supportive, loving, and behind her 100%. If she asks for help, by all means give it; just be sure your comments are directed at the work, not at her.

Friendships are becoming increasingly important to your child at ten and eleven. Her art skills will be strengthened and she will be greatly encouraged if some of her friends are interested in art too. If you don't know of any other children interested in art, ask your child's teacher if she knows of a child who likes to do the same kind of artwork as your child. Then invite her over. It wouldn't really matter if the child was a year younger or older, just so she is artistic too. One of my best students in fourth grade was this way. Mary would spend hours drawing, while her classmates would be working on other projects like science, math, or computers. They would say to her, "Mary, come over here and work with us." She would usually say no and continue to work on her drawing. I know this made her feel uncomfortable, because she was the only one in the room who liked artwork almost to the exclusion of everything else. You may have noticed this in your child too. It will help her be more comfortable with her talent if she knows there are other children like herself. She will not need to have all her friends be artists, but one or two would be very encouraging.

This is a good age to take your child on small "visually-oriented" trips. She might enjoy bringing a friend. The trip can be an all-day excursion or just an hour. Artwork can be found in your local bank, library, and historical museum. You and your child might also go to art museums, art fairs, and art galleries. Other museums like the aquarium, planetarium, and arboretum are also good for artistic children. A trip to an aquarium or even a local pet shop, for example, will show your child that a fish is not just an oval body with fins and a tail; fish have many variations. Your child's new interest in the outside world is a good time to help her learn to look closely and discover all its magnificent details.

The more your child looks at her world the better she will be able to reproduce it in artwork. Even on daily trips, point out all the different styles of homes, the different kinds of trees, even the shapes of the clouds. Perhaps she has already pointed these things out to you. A rare few children have the natural gift of an endless curiosity with the way the world looks. No one has taught them to appreciate it. They have always been delighted with the world's beauty. Most of us have to be taught how to see it. I cannot remember if I was that way or if my parents taught me, but I am grateful to them for my endless fascination with the way this world of ours looks. Although my father is gone now, I can still hear him call out to me as he did so often when I was a little girl, "Donna, come here, hurry, come on, hurry up or you'll miss it! See up there, look, do you see the squirrel, look at those cheeks, they're full of acorns. Doesn't he look funny the way his cheeks are puffed out!" Whether you take your child on a long trip or go around the corner, keep her looking and talking about everything she sees, and she will use that visual knowledge in all her artwork.

At age ten and eleven your child will have many friends. Invite her friends to join in her art projects and go along on field trips. Be watchful of criticism of her artwork by friends and family and help her understand their remarks. This is a good age—their art skills will be better than ever before, and many new art media can be tried with relative success.

Below are a few projects your ten and eleven year old might enjoy trying.

Calligraphy

At ten and eleven many of my students enjoyed learning "fancy writing" or calligraphy. To get your child started, purchase just one calligraphy felt-tipped pen. If she likes it, you can get a full set. To learn how to make each letter, she can check out a book at the library or purchase a pamphlet at an art supply store. You might encourage her by requesting that she write special quotations on index cards, do the lettering on your invitations, print your name on the mail box, letter a "for sale" sign, or help you make a poster. She could also embellish the lettering with geometric, floral, leaf, or animal designs. Not every child enjoys calligraphy, but those who like it are usually very enthusiastic. If your child enjoys this, she will probably need some instruction through a good teacher, or a video, or by reading books on the subject.

Outer Space Collage

Have your child create a picture of what she thinks it will be like in outer space in the future. Encourage her to use other things on her artwork besides the usual colored pencils, markers, and paints. She might use glitter, silver paper, aluminum foil, wire or even paper clips to make the stars and spaceships.

Using different materials on one picture makes it a collage. One of my students cut out magazine photographs that had blue in them to create her sky. She tore each paper into different sizes and shapes, then glued them into the area where she wanted it to be a sky. The sky had an almost eerie quality.

Contour Drawings

Up till now, your child has probably been learning to draw by looking at other people's drawings, photographs, or through books. There is another way that may produce a great improvement in her drawing skills, called contour drawing. This kind of drawing is usually done from real-life settings. As she draws, she will look more at the object that at her paper.

The first thing you need is something to draw. I usually start my students with a flower. Set it in front of your child and let her draw it for no more than five minutes. Put this picture away. Now have her draw it again, but this time have her draw the flower without looking at her paper, just looking at the contour of the object. This drawing will look more like scribbles than a flower, but that is okay. Get a new piece of paper and draw it again, only this time look at the paper only twice. Do this about five times, each time increasing the number of times she can look at the paper. Each drawing should only take five to ten minutes. After she has competed eight drawings, tell her to make one more drawing of it, remembering that it is more important to look at *what* she is drawing than at the paper. Now compare the last drawing to the very first drawing. She should see a great deal of improvement.

Art teachers have taught thirty- and forty-year-old people how to draw who have never drawn before, by using the contour method. She can learn it on her own, but if you can find a teacher who will teach contour drawing, this is an excellent age to start.

Sculpture

Clay sculpture is an instant hit with most ten- and eleven-year-old kids. They will enjoy almost any kind of clay; you can even reintroduce salt clay. They now have enough coordination to make some beautiful sculptures.

Your child will especially enjoy making sculptures out of papier maché. Large shapes can be made by first bending heavy wire into the basic shape, then wrapping newspaper around all of the wire and securing it with string or masking tape. Place extra newspaper around the sections you want to be larger than the rest. For example, in making a dog, put extra layers of paper over the chest, neck, and upper leg areas. Place strips of paper approximately 1" x 6" in diluted white glue and drape over the body until the whole body is covered with at least five layers of paper. Allow the papier maché to dry and then paint it. You can use sandpaper to smooth the rough edges. Papier maché objects are surprisingly strong and will last a very long time. My papier maché purple and pink polka-dotted dog Priscilla that my mom saved for many years was a big hit at my graduate level art education class, but as fate would have it, Priscilla was laid to rest at age thirty-five after being attacked by wild things in the attic.

There are a lot of different sculpture media on the market, so let your child try as many as you can afford. If she would like to try carving, you might get a cube of soft carving material. There are many clays on the market that will harden in the oven and can then be painted. Sculptures can also be made with wire, cloth, and assorted found items.

Sculpture classes are hard to find, mainly because of the mess involved in making sculptures of any type. Be sure your child realizes that she must keep the work area clean or you may lose patience and have to make her quit. A good sculptor, as well as a good painter, cleans her tools and washes down the work area before she quits. This often involves quitting before she is ready. Insist that she keep the area clean and tidy and give her lots of praise. Of course, if she doesn't, you have two choices: you can clean it yourself or take away the privilege of working on sculptures. Or, as my friend Bette did with her husband, banish him to one of the far corners of the basement where the mess cannot be seen.

Sculpture is a fascinating art form. If your child likes it, do all you can to encourage her. Our cities, office buildings, gardens, and homes need more good sculptures.

Posters

Your child will probably be asked to do posters, especially if she can draw well. Posters are actually very difficult. She will need to use every principle of good design to make the poster do what it is supposed to do: promote a candidate, sell an idea, invite people to attend a function, or support a cause. When your child is asked to make a poster, first she needs to think of the words she will use, then sketch her ideas on scrap paper and finally organize them into an attractive layout to fit on poster board. The way a poster is designed is just as important as how well it is drawn.

A simple way to get a good layout for the poster is to use an ad from a newspaper or magazine and imitate that layout. For example, if the ad had large lettering at the top of the page, she might want to do that too. If the advertisement had one large object covering the entire page, she might draw her picture over the whole poster. If the ad had a decorative border she might put one on the poster. After she has imitated a few professional magazine ads, she will be able to create her own layout designs.

A good poster is easy to read, attractive to the eye, neat, and makes its point thoroughly and quickly. The library, art supply stores, and bookstores also have some good books that show kids how to make good posters.

Paper Mosaics

A mosaic is a picture made of small pieces of stone or glass. You see them quite often in large churches and old government buildings. Stained glass windows are a kind of mosaic. Paper mosaics can be quite beautiful too.

For this project, she will make a paper mosaic. First, have your child sketch a picture on a piece of dark paper with a light colored pencil. Instead of coloring it, glue down small, colored squares of paper. A paper mosaic takes a great deal of time to complete, so use a small piece of the dark paper for the first project. She might begin with a 5" x 7" paper and glue down squares that are 1/4" to 1/2". A mosaic is put down much like wall or floor tile, with a small space in between each piece; the pieces should not overlap. The paper squares can come from all different sources. I have seen beautiful results using wallpaper, photographs from magazines, and even pieces of fabric. With this project your child will really appreciate some help. If you and your child would like to do one with ceramic tile on an old coffee table, you can purchase the supplies from art catalogs (see Appendix).

Introduction to Colorful Painting

This is a good time to introduce making colors by mixing different paints together. This project will have your child create three different sets of colors. The first will use one color plus white, the second will use one color plus black, and the third will mix one color with another. Your child will probably feel like a chemist after she has finished this project.

Using a long strip of paper, have her paint as many different tints of a single color as will fit on the strip of paper. The more she makes, the better she understands the immense range of colors possible. Tints are made by adding white to a color. Let her do this to all the colors: red, yellow, blue, green, orange, purple, brown, and black. She should try to make as many different tints as possible.

After she has made them, she can then do the same thing, but this time add black to each color and make *shades*. She'll probably find she can make a lot more tints of one color than she can shades.

For a final project, have her do the same thing only she should put her paint on strips after mixing one color with another. For example, a little blue added to red with a touch of white will make a rose color. Blue and red with a touch of black will create a burgundy or maroon color. This can be a very interesting project.

Supplies she will need are: a lot of clean water, paper towels, wax paper or plastic plate for mixing colors, a paint brush, and acrylic or tempera paint (do not use watercolors). If your child enjoyed this project, she may want to try painting a picture or even taking painting lessons. Be sure she saves the color strips, so she will be reminded of just how many different colors she can use in paintings.

PROJECTS FOR CHILDREN AGES 12 AND 13

Your child will probably continue to be social and have close friends when he is twelve and thirteen years old. This is a good age to take art-related trips to museums, art shows, and galleries. Your artistic child needs time alone to develop his talent, but as he approaches twelve and thirteen he will want to spend an increasing amount of time with his friends. To keep his love for art alive and developing, encourage friendships with other children who like to do artwork. You might ask his art teacher to recommend someone. If there is no one your child would even remotely consider befriending, you might consider enrolling him in an art class. Students who are talented in music have friends in the band, but often a child who loves to paint and draw is left by himself. Encourage your child to share his love for art with all his friends. Even if they aren't interested at the time, they may find his enthusiasm for art enlightening.

This is the age at which he may quit doing artwork altogether, but I wouldn't necessarily worry about it. If he truly loves artwork, he will soon miss it. Offer him art classes and ask him to do things around the house that will use his talent. You might ask him to make a garage sale sign, help you select a new picture for the living room, make a greeting card, paint your name on your mail box, make a family photo collage, or even help you select new clothes.

Praise and encouragement are vital to a twelve and thirteen year old. He may take the criticism you give his artwork as a personal attack. Whenever you offer advice, it is important to stress that you are not unhappy with him, but are simply commenting on what he is doing. When you discuss his artwork, you will encourage his skill development more if you talk mainly about what he has done *well*. If you give him a chance, he will probably tell you what he needs to work on. You, however, do not want him to rely on praise from you as his only source of encouragement. He needs to learn how to encourage and praise himself.

> *The advantage of doing one's praising for oneself is that one can lay it on so thick and exactly in the right places.*
> Samuel Butler, *The Way of All Flesh*

At age twelve and thirteen, for many kids, neatness has become a thing of the past, especially in their rooms. Although your child may be going through a messy stage, he needs to realize that his artwork has to be neat or people will not look at it. You may have to help him understand this by rejecting work that has stains, smudges, or is on crumpled paper. Explain to him what you like about his artwork, but do not hang it up. This may seem harsh, but neatness in artwork has got to be established or your child will not understand its rejection by his friends, teachers, and eventually his customers.

This is a good age to let him try different media. You might give him a certain amount of money each month for buying art supplies. An art supply catalog will give him a good idea of what is available. It is also a good time to introduce him to power tools, the sewing machine, the video camera, and computer art.

A twelve or thirteen year old will be able to work on an art project for several days. He will also want to spend spend periods of time drawing in great detail. Some of my students would spend months drawing just the head of a horse. This is a good age for them to concentrate on developing their drawing skills, because they are finally coordinated and focused enough to work for long periods of time. A man once told that the best learning comes after three hours of steady work at it, and I am inclined to agree with him.

If your child is interested in one medium and does not want to learn another, offer to get him other kinds of art materials but do not insist. If he has found a medium he truly loves, provide the best art supplies you can afford, take trips to see other artists' work, offer lessons, and buy books on the subject. One of my best art students, Carley, was already doing oil paintings at age eleven. She loved it to the exclusion of all other media. By concentrating on oil painting for three years, she was able to create pictures of almost professional quality by eighth grade.

This is a good age to get your child an art magazine subscription. Most magazines have articles about artists' materials and contemporary artists, how the artist can improve his techniques, new projects, and will show him art from the past. A magazine subscription would be a great encouragement to your child.

Constructing and Building with Cardboard

Teens really enjoy this project because they have such success with it. To make a building, the artist must first determine the scale. If 1' of actual building height will 1" of cardboard, that would mean that a 10' foot high house would be 10" tall. If you want the cardboard house to be bigger, you could have a ratio of 1' to 2". Before you begin cutting the cardboard, sketch out the idea and make a paper model. Cardboard from boxes works well for the walls because it is inexpensive and easy to cut with a razor blade or scissors. One mistake most of my students made was in the placement of windows and doors. These are usually in line with each other at the top. A flat, heavy piece of cardboard makes a good base and will keep the sides from collapsing. Your child might add a gravel path, bushes, grass, trees, cellophane for windows, and even a mail box. After doing this project, several of my students discovered they wanted to be architects. This is a project your child may enjoy doing with a friend.

Embroidery

One year I took a chance and introduced my favorite craft of embroidery to my twelve- and thirteen-year-old students. It was a huge success. Their first project was to do the alphabet in cross-stitch. Before they began, they copied an alphabet made especially for cross-stitch onto graph paper by putting an "X" in every square in which there was to be a cross-stitch. Then they were given a 6" embroidery hoop, a piece of prewashed Aida cloth, a needle, and some embroidery thread.

Color is important in embroidery. The threads come in well over a hundred colors and choosing the right ones for this project can be very difficult. If your child doesn't know which colors of thread to use, he should first pick out three colors that he likes. Then pick one more. Hold up the four together and see if they all look good together. If he is not sure, ask him if one color jumps out. If it does, put it back and choose another. Keep doing this until he is happy with his selection of colors. Try not to influence your child's choices; each of us has his own color preferences. Place the Aida cloth in the hoop and let him begin stitching. Some students put a border around the project when they were finished. The squares of cloth were then laundered and put in frames or made into pillows. Embroidery is a good project to do with a friend because once you get started, it doesn't require a great deal of concentration.

Movie with a Video Camera

Let your child try his hand at making a movie with a video camera. He may want to enlist other members of the family or his friends. After he has decided on a story, he needs to draw it on a story board. The hardest part of making a movie is to think of the story not in words but in visual terms. A story board is a series of approximately twenty-five boxes on paper. In each box, the artist sketches a scene of the movie he is about to create. On this story board, he will have to decide where it will be filmed, what kind of clothes the actors will wear, how he will get the message across, when it will occur, and most important, why he is making the movie. The story board should answer the questions who, what, when, where, why, and how. Once this is decided, he can begin filming. If your child really enjoys this art form, let him take a video class or get him a book on making movies with a home video camera.

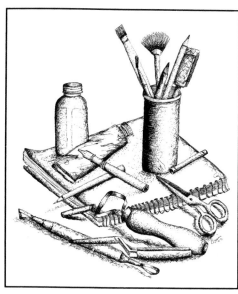

Cary A. Cody

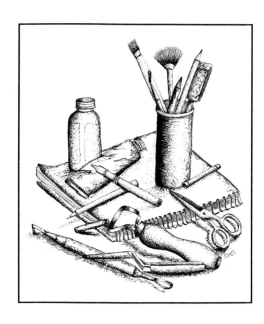

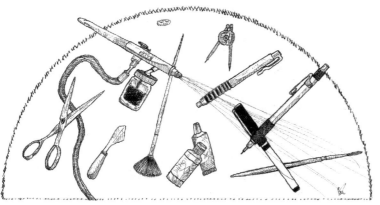

Painting

If your child has not worked with paints before, he should first try the painting project in the section for ten and eleven year olds. The easiest kind of paint to work with is acrylics, but they are relatively expensive, and unless your child has done a lot of painting, tempera paint is a good alternative. He will also need a medium-weight paper, good paint brushes, a mixing tray or piece of wax paper, several containers of water, and a rag. His first painting project might be a design emphasizing the many ways to use a paint brush. He can make dashes, thin wavy lines, crisscrossed lines, up and down strokes, circles, and any other kind of line he can think of. One of my better art students painted ten different lines on each of five sheets of paper. They were painted in rows much as you would do if you were writing. He came up with fifty different ways to make a line. We taped the five sheets together and hung it on the wall—it looked fantastic.

Next, have him try painting a single object. It might be a Raggedy Ann doll, a vase, or a piece of fruit. Be sure he gives it a setting; for example, it might be on a table, outside, or in a window. Encourage him to use some of the same brush strokes he used in his first painting. In the next painting, let him try painting three objects. This kind of painting is called a *still life*.

Painting is very difficult, and your child's first attempts may be very discouraging. Remind him that if he will practice, he can get better. When talking about his paintings find at least one thing that is really nice, even if it is just a color, and compliment him. Provide a lot of paper and good paints, display his work, be sure he keeps the painting area and tools clean and neat, and compliment his effort as well as his work.

Flicker Books

Back when animated cartoons were first invented, children could purchase flicker books. They consisted of a tablet with approximately fifty pages, on each of which was a slightly different cartoon drawing. Using your thumb, you were to flip through the pages quickly and watch the drawings appear to move. On each page was a drawing almost exactly like the one on the preceding page. For example, if Mickey Mouse was waving, the position of his hand would be at a slightly different angle on each page. The faster you flipped through the book, the faster his hand would wave. Your child will love making a flicker book of his own. An easy one to begin with is a bouncing ball. In order to see the position of the ball on the previous page, use paper that is translucent. To have an even movement of the ball, make the ball on each page just slightly above the one on the previous page. Be sure he makes all the drawings on the bottom half of the tablet. This will allow for a place to hold onto as the pages are flipped. Many of my students would try to make their books with notebook paper, but they were invariably disappointed with the results. In order for the pages to flip in a constant rhythm, the bottom edges must be perfectly square. Purchase paper pads that are secured together at the top. Print shops usually have them for sale extra cheap. Some of the flicker books my students made were about shipwrecks, a racing car, a basketball, a man walking a dog, swimmers, divers, a person waving good-bye, and a dog chasing a cat.

Sculpture

By now, your child has probably made a few sculptures. This is a good time to let him take lessons. If he still wants to work on his own or you can't find a sculpture class, you might purchase a soft carving brick or clay that will harden in the oven. He will need a few carving tools and a plastic or metal decorating wheel. Other materials for sculpture he might like to try are wire, plaster, bass and balsa wood, or even cloth to make soft sculpture. Instructions for using these materials are usually found in their containers or in books or pamphlets. If he would like to work with a friend, you might suggest they make a project together. As he develops his ability to make sculptures, he will also develop a better understanding of how to draw.

Colored Pencil Drawings

If your child loves to draw, you might invest in a good set of colored pencils. Some of the cheaper varieties have very hard lead and it is difficult, if not impossible, to get bright, rich colors. A good set of colored pencils will last a long time, especially if your child takes good care of them. Get him a hand-held pencil sharpener, so he will be less likely to break the lead when he sharpens it. He can also use a sharp knife; some artists think this gives a stronger point.

Before he begins a picture, encourage him to try making rows of different kinds of lines as discussed in the section on Painting on page 97. Encourage him to make other colors by placing one color over another or colors next to each other. For example, if he is drawing a portrait and his only brown pencil is too light, you might suggest that he use black lines over and next to the brown for a darker effect. Colored pencils are a natural medium for children. They have been using pencils for many years and, by this age, are very adept with them.

There are several different varieties of colored pencils. One is charcoal, which requires special paper, erasers, and a fixative to keep the picture from smearing. Another kind allows him to add water to the pencils to give the drawing a watercolor effect. Both varieties can be enjoyed by your child, but for your child's first set, he will probably most enjoy a set of soft-leaded colored pencils.

If he cannot think of anything to draw, you might suggest one of the following:

- portrait of a family member
- a tree as it changes with the seasons
- a pattern for a quilt
- outer space—2200 A.D.
- your dream home
- your dream husband or wife
- your favorite cartoon character talking to _____
- divide the entire paper into squares and put something different but related in some way in each square
- make a fancy sign for your room, the bathroom, or the front door
- cut a photograph of a famous painting in half and, using only one of the halves, paint the other half
- draw an insect from memory or from life
- photograph a sunset, then paint it
- make a picture in which the border is just as important as the main image

PROJECTS FOR YOUNG ADULTS
AGES 14 TO 18

Kids at this age are no longer children, so I will refer to them as young adults or teens. If your teen has been creating since she was very young, she has probably found one art medium that she enjoys above all others. Encourage her to work as much as possible in the art form in which she has the most talent and interest, but allow her to branch out and take other art classes. If she has always loved painting, a good sculpture or printing class will help her understand what it takes to make a good painting. There is a correlation between all the art media, and it seems the more you know about one, the better you understand the others.

Between the ages of fourteen and eighteen, your teen will be very busy taking academic classes, and she may not be able to take an art class every semester, but try at least to have her involved in a school activity in which she can use her art skills and talent. You might encourage her to submit a cartoon to the school newspaper, enter local art contests, take private lessons, enroll in a woodshop or sewing class, work on or organize a school poster committee, join the video/photography club, help compile the school yearbook, provide decorations for school parades and dances, or even run a small business making and selling items she has made with the school insignia on them. Every time she works on a project that uses her art skills, she will develop a broader understanding of art.

Friendships will continue to be very important to your teenager. Many educators fail to make use in their classes of teens' deep love and need for one another to enhance learning. Encourage your teen to work with a friend or two on some of her art projects. As they work and discuss their projects, they will teach each other art skills and techniques, inspire one another, develop a better understanding of the concept that art is communication, and become less self-conscious about the quality of their work. My late husband attended Hershey School for boys, and told me when he was a teenager the boys would all study together. He felt he learned more because the older boys explained concepts in a different way than the teacher did. Competition with each other also stimulated his desire to excel. Invite your teen's artistic friends over and encourage them to work together. Talk to them about what they are going to do and invite them to show you what they have done before they go home.

Friendships come easily for some teenagers, while others need a little encouragement. My friend Jean found out through the high school art teacher that her daughter always sat with a girl she was sure was her best friend. Jean said she had never met her. Jean wanted to meet this new friend, so she went to the art supply store and purchased several kits for making designer jewelry, and then suggested that her daughter invite someone over to help her. Although she was hesitant, the daughter realized her mother went to a lot of expense and trouble, so she asked her friend over. They had a great time and after ten years are still best friends. Friendships are very important to your teenager. She needs friends to help develop her sense of self, to broaden her knowledge of the way others outside her family fit into our world, and with whom she can share her love for art. Learning can be more exciting and challenging when it is shared with a friend.

Quality art materials will be a great help to your teenager as she begins to "fine tune" her art skills. My son Lee came up to me about halfway through his painting class and asked if he could use some of my paint brushes because the hair was falling out of his brushes. I was grateful that he asked because without the good paint brushes, I might not have received the beautiful fall landscape now hanging in my living room. The simpler, less expensive art materials used in elementary school are just not appropriate anymore. Your teen will be working harder and longer on her projects. If her materials are cheap, they will fall apart and may ultimately discourage her. Talk to her art teacher about the kind of supplies she needs and purchase the best materials you can afford. Amy, one of my students, began painting in sixth grade and continued to paint seriously until high school. Her parents decided that such dedication deserved a present, so they asked me what they should purchase to help her with her painting. I asked if Amy had an easel and they said no. When I explained the advantages of working at an easel instead of a desk, they decided to surprise her with a new easel that weekend. Having an easel meant she could stand while she was painting, she could step back and look at her work easily, lighting was less of a problem, and she could paint much larger pictures. Whether you purchase a new easel, a set of quality brushes, some high quality paper, or new sculpture tools, your teen's artistic ability will be greatly encouraged when you purchase good quality materials.

At fourteen or fifteen, your teen might enjoy taking art lessons from a professional. She can take private lessons or night classes at your community center or junior college. Some of my art students enjoyed a summer art camp especially for high school students, given at a nearby university. This can be expensive, but a great deal of learning occurs when you can spend all day working on it.

If you think your teen works well enough on her own, you might consider getting her an art teacher who will work on a consulting basis. As your child comes to a problem that she cannot figure out, she can schedule an appointment with the art teacher. As your young adult's skills develop, she can get assistance with design problems and technical skills from a variety of sources: teachers, friends, magazines, books, viewing other artists' work, and the employees or manager at the art supply store.

Your teenager may have just developed an interest in art and may be concerned that she will be behind the other students. This may be true, but keep in mind, now that your teen is older she can learn new things quickly, especially if she has a strong desire to work hard. A lot of art "talent" is just plain, old-fashioned hard work. I didn't begin working in art until I was a senior in high school. Although my mother was an artist all her life, I only watched her paint, never really wanting to create artwork myself. While in my senior year in high school, I had the opportunity to choose an elective for the fall semester. I heard the girls talking about this "fantastic" art teacher everyone loved. He was firm yet gentle, adored his students, and not only taught you about art but sat down with each of his students and made sure they knew how to do each project. I asked my parents if they thought I should give it a try, and they both agreed an art class for one semester might not only be a good idea but would probably be fun. To my surprise, a whole new area of interest was opened up to me. This one simple art class opened the door to a lifetime of wonderful hobbies, an increased awareness of the beauty of the world around me, and several careers. Because I was older, I was able to (almost) catch up with my peers by the end of my senior year. If your child is just starting to do art in her teens, do not make her feel as though she is too late. Even Grandma Moses was a late bloomer—she began painting after age sixty. Be supportive of your child's new interest, but wait to purchase expensive materials until she decides which art medium she likes best.

Below is a list of art projects for fourteen- to eighteen-year-old students. They are written to your young adult directly because suggestions from parents, at this age, aren't always welcome. You might make a copy of the projects and post it on the bulletin board in her studio. Most of the projects can be finished in a day or two, and are designed to help your young adult better understand the principles of design, develop her ability to think in visual terms, and improve the overall quality of her artwork. Your teen will also enjoy a copy of Chapter 4, "Art Terminology."

Geometric Shapes

Take a famous painting and place a sheet of tracing paper over it. Trace the picture, but instead of drawing it in the same style as the artist, break each part of the picture into simple geometric shapes. This is also fun to do to a photograph of a famous sculpture.

Punny Pictures

Recall your favorite pun and turn it into a picture or sculpture. A "pun," according to the *Random House College Dictionary*, is "... the humorous use of a word or combinations of words so as to emphasize the different meanings or applications, or the use of words that are alike or nearly alike in sound but different in meaning. A play on words." For example: you could create a humorous picture using the phrase "a hero sandwich" by placing your favorite comic strip hero between two pieces of bread. Other puns that would easily translate into drawings are: "She accidentally learned the traffic laws" or "It was a well-read book."

Logos

Find ten logos in newspapers and magazines that you think are outstanding. Copy them onto paper at least twice the original size. Index cards work well. Most logos are designed by professional artists and are beautiful works of art in their own right. After you have completed copying your ten logos, make one for a company you or your family might own in the future. If you enjoy this project, try to copy fifty, or if you are really ambitious, copy a hundred. Two years ago I had my students working on this project for a full year. We all learned a great deal. It seems that if you really want to learn how to draw something well, you will accomplish your goal if you just hang in there and do it a hundred times. I realize this is a lot of drawing, but give it a try sometime and see if it isn't true.

Photo Collage I

Go through an old magazine and tear out all the photographs that you like. It is important not to let anyone else choose the pictures. Then find one thing that they all have in common; it may be a color, the subject matter, or the mood or emotional quality of the photograph.

To make the collage, cut out the most important part of each photograph, arrange the pieces into an interesting composition, and then glue them onto a piece of paper. Your theme will be clarified if you include the word describing it as part of the collage. To preserve your work, put the picture between two pieces of clear Contact® paper.

Photo Collage II

National Geographic magazines work well for this kind of collage. If you do not have any, you can find them at garage sales and library book sales.

This collage involves taking two photographs that have something in common and superimposing one over another. The finished picture will look like two pictures in one. The pictures need to be related in some way. For example, I found two photographs that had similar colors and a related theme. The largest one was a picture of an Oriental rice field and the other a portrait of an old farmer. I cut the portrait to one-half the width of the landscape but kept the same height. This is very important. When you have found your two pictures, cut the smaller picture into $1/4$" strips. Your strips should be the same height as the larger picture; you are actually cutting the width. Spread the strips out so they will cover the entire width of the larger photograph by leaving a space approximately $1/4$" between each of the strips and carefully glue them in place. When finished, look at your picture from about 4 feet away and you will be able to see both pictures. Some pictures even have an animated quality. To give the pictures more stability, you can glue them onto stiff paper before arranging, cutting, and gluing them together.

Variations of a Single Color

For this project use colored pencils, paints, or pastels. The object is to color in a design using the same color in many variations.

Use tints, shades, and blends of only one color. For example, if you use blue in your design, make many blues by using differing amounts of black, white, brown, yellow, red, orange, green, and purple with the blue. For this project, be sure the color blue is still predominant. You can use a design of your own, one from a book, or graph paper. You might also texture an area on your design or make the color in different intensities.

Illustrate a Children's Book

Make a gift for a young child that he will always treasure by illustrating and writing a children's book. You might do an old traditional story like "The Three Little Pigs," make up a story, or design a simple counting or ABC book for a preschooler. Sketch your ideas on scrap paper before you work on the final paper to be sure the illustrations and text are correct.

The book itself can simply be fastened together with paper fasteners, folded in half, and sewn down the middle with heavy string or yarn, or crease all the pages accordion-style. The illustrations might be done in colored pencil, paint, or you can even make it a collage.

My eighth graders made story books for the kindergartners one year. Instead of drawing all the pictures, one student used potato prints for the leaves, flowers, and trees and drew in the people in her story about the jungle. The kindergartners showed their gratitude with big smiles, hugs, and many ooohs and aaahs. A handmade gift is always treasured.

Improve Your Handwriting

This is a great age to improve your penmanship. Many think beautiful writing is done mainly by women, but some of the best penmanship, I have found, is by men. Learning calligraphy can also be a good way to improve your personal image. Every time you write, you will be proud of the way it looks, and this may ultimately reflect upon how you see yourself. Beautiful handwriting is like giving yourself and the people who have read it a "warm fuzzy." You think enough of yourself and them to write in a manner that is not only easy to read but beautiful to look at.

You may have to get rid of some bad habits, so it may take about three months of steady practice and then a year or two of conscious effort until the new style of penmanship comes naturally.

The next step beyond beautiful handwriting is calligraphy. It is done with special pens and in a specific manner. There are inexpensive felt calligraphy pen sets for beginners, which you can purchase in any art or craft store. There are also a number of good books and pamphlets on calligraphy to help you learn how to make the letters.

Hair Styles

Take a school picture that you don't want anymore and cut out just the face, neck, and shoulders. This may be a scary sight, but don't worry. You will be designing new hair styles for it in this assignment. Tape the picture to a piece of paper and try coloring in different hair styles and even different hair colors. Release the tape and move your photo to another area of the paper and try another hair style. If you have a full-length picture of yourself, you can also try different clothing styles. The more you experiment with hair and clothing styles, the better you will realize that what looks good on one person doesn't always look good on you.

A fashion scrapbook is an interesting way to find your clothing style. Collect pictures of clothing styles you love from magazines, and do not let your friends or parents influence your opinion. Put the pictures in a scrapbook and when you have fifty pages, examine them and you will find your preference in clothing. You might discover that you like not only a particular style but specific colors and textures.

If you enjoy this project you might suggest that your parents purchase for you a good book or two on fashion and hair design. There is a lot of work and creativity in fashion design that most people do not realize until they actually start talking about and working on projects.

Still Life

Create a still life of all the paraphernalia used in your favorite sport. Arrange all the equipment in one area and then draw it, showing the quiet contemplation of an athlete before the big game.

You can draw it, paint it, or try your hand at photography. Try different kinds of lighting on your still life: above, below, and at different angles. It's important to keep a record of the lighting you used if you are photographing it, so you will remember what you did when the photographs are developed. You may think you will re-member, but time has a way of confusing even the smartest people.

Your still life will need an appropriate background. I once saw a sports still life that used a mirror in the background, which had a reflection of a young man in his uniform sitting on his bed praying for a safe and successful game. Some other backgrounds might have a window with other athletes outside, wallpaper with sports-related designs, a door slightly open with someone looking in, or a bulletin board with souvenirs.

Some important points in making a good still life are: have at least one thing that is very large and one that is very small; put in shadows; one object should be the focal point that leads you into the picture; have a variety of textures; make sure the viewer's eye never leaves the picture; detail adds interest; and be sure there is strong contrast somewhere in the drawing, whether it is in the way you draw it or in the objects themselves. A still life can be a very moving and impressive picture if time is taken to do it well.

House Portraits

Here's a chance to give someone a gift they will always trea-sure: a picture of his or her house. In our homes, we are sheltered, loved, fed; we rest and entertain ourselves and our friends. A pic-ture, painting, or even a small sculpture of someone's home is a gift he will treasure. When I lived near Chicago, I sold house portraits in a local store. Most of the people were giving them to their parents or a special friend. I created the house portraits in embroidery. Some artists earn their living selling them. They can be done in wa-tercolor, pen and ink, charcoal, oil paints, pastels, or clay.

The first step in creating a house portrait is to make a sketch. If at all possible, make a personal visit to the home. In this sketch, get the proper measurements by using graph paper and a ruler. To mea-sure the height of the house, hold a ruler about 12" from your eyes, then measure the height of the house as it appears on the ruler. Write down this measurement and sketch it onto the graph paper. Do this for every part of the house. For example, the ruler might say the total height of the house is 4", the roof is $1^3/4$" high and 5" long, etc. Put all the measurements on the graph paper. Be sure to mea-sure the height (from the ground), width, and length of all the win-dows and doors. Many a good house portrait is ruined by improper placement of the windows and doors. Also be sure to mark where the yard and sky meet in relation to the house. A good sketch is crucial to your final picture. For your final paper, put a border of masking tape that covers about ¹/₂" of the paper, mark the center of the paper, and then draw the house as light as you possibly can until you get it just right. Finish it in paints, colored pencil, ink, etc. You will probably be working on it for a long time, so, to keep the paper clean, be sure you rest your hand on a piece of stiff paper. Also be sure to cover the work when you are done working on it each day. House portraits are difficult to do but the rewards are many.

House portraits can be financially rewarding, a good way to make a lot of people happy, and a real adventure. If you enjoy doing them, with a little practice you may be able to sell them. A few hints from years of mistakes: when making a picture, be sure to leave a ¹/₂" border so it will fit properly into a frame; include the name and address somewhere in the picture; and be sure to include something in the picture that lets the viewer know people are living inside; for example, a newspaper, a potted plant, a curtain brushed aside, an open window, or a pet.

Tree Branch

Next time you go outside look for unusual-shaped tree branches. They should be approximately 12" long. The more unusual the shape, the better. To turn the tree branch into an art object, add things to it, cut and shape it, or just clean off the bark. Work with it until you find an interesting shape, a creature, or a familiar manmade object. You might add other pieces of wood, paint, nails, yarn, etc. Now that you have developed more advanced art skills, you will be surprised how well a simple project like this will turn out.

Copy a Photograph

Find a black-and-white photograph of something or someone you really like or admire. You are going to make an exact copy of it. There are several ways to do this. One way is to place a transparent grid over the photograph or draw a grid directly onto it. Next, lightly draw another grid on a piece of drawing paper, but make this one at least twice as large as the one on the photograph. Copy the photograph square by square onto the drawing paper. Try not to think about drawing the entire picture, just concentrate on drawing each square one at a time. To help you concentrate, turn your photograph upside down so you won't be distracted by the whole picture.

Photographs can also be copied by placing a piece of transparent paper directly over the original picture and tracing the photograph. You can also project a slide of what you want to draw onto the drawing surface. This is how many artists work when they have to draw a very large picture. The high school insignia on our gym wall was done this way. The artist drew it on regular drawing paper, photographed it, had it made into a slide, then projected the slide onto the gym wall. He then traced it onto the wall and it was ready to be painted. One of my students also did this with the logo for a soft drink company. Her younger sister wanted the logo on her bedroom wall. To draw it as exactly as possible, she used the slide method. With a few adjustments of the slide projector and the slide, she was able to get a $1/2$" soft drink logo to cover 4' of the wall.

One other way to make an exact copy of a picture is just to look at it and make it look as much like the original as possible. The trick here is first to find the middle of the picture and mark it on your drawing paper. Making an exact copy of a photograph or a painting is a good exercise and will help you develop your art skills. If you like doing this, you may want to consider a career in art restoration.

Photo Collage

Instead of putting all your photographs in albums, you might enjoy making a photo collage. Gather up some of your photos and cut out only the part of each picture that is the most meaningful to you. Purchase a large frame with glass and use the cardboard backing as a base for your photo collage. Arrange the photographs before you glue them down. The collage needs to employ all the elements of good design if it is to look professional. Here are a few tips: use one picture that is quite a bit larger than the others for your center of interest; use at least three pictures that are very small as accents; include some writing or numbers (dates, addresses, names) somewhere in your composition; be sure your arrangement has a good eye flow around the picture; be sure there is nothing in the photos that will lead your eye out of the picture; and repeat one thing over and over throughout the design. This is a good way to apply and better understand the design principles, as well as a good way to get those cherished photos out of the albums and onto the walls so everyone can enjoy them.

Scrap Metal Collage

We live around metal objects, yet rarely do we notice their inherent beauty. In this project you can create a metal collage using a wide range of old metal objects and mounting them on a piece of wood. Some things you might consider using are rusty nails, washers, chain, old watch parts, screws, copper pipe, nuts, bolts, hooks, wire, and old door handles. As you are putting it together, remember to use all the elements of good design. The wood that you mount the pieces on can be slick and highly polished or just an old piece of driftwood. Experiment with the placement of the pieces of metal before you secure them to the wood. The glue can be epoxy, silicone, or from a glue gun. Corrosion of metal creates some beautiful shades of blue, green, brown, orange, and black.

I have been collecting old watch parts for years and hope someday to put them into a collage. A metal collage can also be very large, but you may need help from someone who has knowledge of welding techniques. Keep in mind the rules of design apply here too. The metal collage should have a theme; use one large item and a few that are very small; use a variety of textures; repeat one object at least three times, etc. You might hang your metal collage in your family room, in a work area, over the garage, or on a porch.

FINAL COMMENTS FOR ALL AGE GROUPS

As a parent, you want to help your child. You especially want to give him just the right amount of help, not too much or too little. Parenting is not easy and there are few pat answers. Listen to your child and watch his behavior. He will probably tell you when you are helping too much or too little. For example, he might tell you quite honestly, "Mom, I want to it all by myself now," or if he needs some help he might say, "These scissors just won't cut." Another sign of you helping too much is over-dependence—not wanting to do anything without you.

Watch his behavior. Anger or irritation while working on an art project may mean that it is too hard for him. As a young parent, I always wanted my child to try something just beyond his abilities. Quite often I would have to put the whole project away for six months because my child just did not understand it or did not have the coordination to complete it. The project was upsetting and frustrating my normally happy child. Watch your child as he does art projects. If you are doing most of it, if he is continually misbehaving, or if he gets bored with it, the project may be beyond his abilities. Wait a few months and introduce it again.

Remind your child that art is communication. Sometimes the message in his artwork will be simply "the beauty of color" or it may be more specific like "deer sleep in the tall grass during the daytime for protection from their enemies." Each art project your child completes is better if the person looking at it either understands the artist's message or the work itself arouses in the viewer an emotion, a thought, or a memory. When your child does not communicate anything to his audience, he has failed. When your child presents his finished artwork, tell him what the project is communicating to you and challenge him to work on his project until his message and your understanding are similar.

Each project in this chapter was designed for independent working; however, you can help your child by collecting and purchasing the materials, encouraging his efforts, demonstrating the proper way to clean up and, especially with the very young, helping him start the project. Parents of artistic children are lucky because their children enjoy working alone most of the time. Your child will, of course, need new challenges, and the projects in this chapter gave you some ideas. There are also many wonderful books in the library with other project ideas for your child.

The most important way for you to encourage your child's art skill development is to provide a space for him to do artwork; materials to do the projects; information on art through books, teachers, and other artists; positive, inspiring words of encouragement; and most important of all, time to do his work.

OUTSTANDING PARENT AWARD

Presented to _____

In the course of encouraging your child to develop his/her artistic talent, and for outstanding efforts in the field of administration, procurement, and loving support, you have furthered your child's artistic talent.

Therefore, this author and your child declare the above-named parent to be most worthy of the title:

❋ *OUTSTANDING PARENT* ❋

Donna B. Gray, Author

_____

Son/Daughter

OUTSTANDING GRANDPARENT AWARD

Presented to _____

In the course of encouraging your grandchild to develop his/her artistic talent, and for outstanding efforts in the field of administration, procurement, and loving support, you have furthered your grandchild's artistic talent.

Therefore, this author and your grandchild declare the above-named grandparent to be most worthy of the title:

❋ *OUTSTANDING GRANDPARENT* ❋

Donna B. Gray, Author

_____

Grandson/Granddaughter

Photocopy this page for your child. Encourage him (when he's ready to present such an award!) to decorate and enhance it any way he likes: re-create it using calligraphy, make a decorative border in any craft or medium, make a special frame.

8.

ART MATERIALS

The art supplies you purchase for a seven year old are quite different from those you buy for a child of fourteen. This chapter will tell you the kind of art supplies to get for your child at a specific age. A good supply of the basic art materials will allow your child to create easily and in a relaxed manner. There is nothing more frustrating for an artist than to have a desire to create something and not have the materials on hand. It is every artists' dream to have a studio full of art supplies, so please try to provide your child with as complete a studio as possible.

The supplies are listed according to the following age groups: 2 to 5, 6 and 7, 8 and 9, 10 and 11, 12 and 13, and 14 to 18. The supplies were chosen by the general physical and mental characteristics of children in each age group as I observed them while teaching school and raising my own children. Your child may be more or less advanced and need supplies from an age group other than his own.

PRICES AND PRICE RANGES

Art supplies can be expensive, and if you aren't careful, you can spend a great deal of money unnecessarily. Local variety stores, for example, now carry art paper, paints, brushes, and other art supplies. Their prices are usually much higher than those of art supply stores and catalog companies. A tablet of drawing paper bought at a variety store will cost almost three times as much as the same one in an art catalog. And a variety store's selection is so limited, you may be forced to buy the wrong kind of supplies, as happened to me several months ago. My grandchildren asked me to buy them a drawing tablet when we were shopping in our local drugstore. We had a choice of two kinds of paper: one was very cheap newsprint and the other was very expensive charcoal drawing paper. Both were overpriced, but I couldn't disappoint my grandchildren. If I had thought ahead, I could have ordered them drawing paper from my art catalog and not only gotten the kind of paper I wanted for them but saved myself some money.

Of all the art supplies, paper is the one that has the most variance in price. The best priced paper of all is free. Working with over 500 art students, I would often get free paper. My art class in Rosedale, Indiana received some beautiful silver paper when a girl's parents were told by some friends that the local printer was throwing rolls of it in the trash. They knew I was looking for paper and immediately drove to the print shop and rescued three huge rolls of gold and silver paper. The classes and I were truly grateful. We used the paper for several years with great enthusiasm. When you consider your time, the cost of driving, and the price of each item, the best prices can often be found through art supply catalog companies. Local art supply stores are also a good source—their prices are a little higher. They are an important asset to your community and a place you can purchase art materials quickly.

There are three basic price ranges for art supplies. The most expensive supplies are usually meant for the professional artist who must use high quality materials. Moderately priced art supplies are perfect for students. Cheap art supplies are rarely recommended. While teaching in the public schools, I have seen many bargain art supplies that look good in September but by December are useless. The most common example is scissors. Out of the 250 primary age students I taught last year, 200 had cheap scissors. My students loved to cut, but their scissors were useless after the first few weeks of school—they would tear the paper more often than cut it. A few other cheap supplies that manufacturers put on the market, in an attempt to outprice the better art supplies, are watercolors (they are so hard you can barely get any color onto the paint brushes), crayons (they are more wax than color), paste (it will not hold and makes a terrible mess), pencils (they are too hard and break easily when sharpened), colored pencils (more clay than pigment and therefore very hard), and erasers that do not completely remove the pencil marks from the paper. Usually the expense of purchasing a better grade of material is made up by its durability and the fact that the child will use it with eagerness and joy, and will have a feeling of accomplishment in the results. In general, you should purchase moderately priced art supplies for your child while she is a young student of art, and as she gets close to professional level, purchase the best.

The art supplies your child needs and wants may turn out to cost a lot of money. Keep in mind that the price is not that much when you compare it to the price of a few good toys, some sports equipment, or a couple of new outfits. Your child will get hundreds of hours of pleasure from just a few basic art supplies. If your budget is small, start out with just a few basic, good quality supplies and slowly build up your child's art supplies each month. I still have paint brushes, palettes, and drawing tools that I used in college well over twenty years ago. Another idea is to purchase the basic supplies like pencils, paper, glue, and crayons for your child and then pay half the cost of any additional supplies. A friend of mine took her son's birthday money from his grandparents and bought him basic art supplies. Then she and her husband put a certain amount aside each month for art materials. The money was put in an envelope and when their son needed new art materials, he could use that money. If there wasn't enough, he would work to earn the rest. The budget idea worked well because it let their son know his parents felt his learning art was important enough to set aside part of their income; he knew the limits of his spending and was therefore extra careful in his selection; and he became a partner with his parents when he helped pay for his art supplies.

ART SUPPLIES FOR CHILDREN AGES 2 TO 5

Children this young have a very small selection of material available to them because of their limited physical abilities and the necessity of purchasing safety-styled materials. These art supplies will consist mainly of paper, crayons, glue, and scissors.

To keep your home organized and clean, you might set aside one place where your child can do her artwork. Tell her that her artwork is to be done there and no place else. Keep all the materials in plastic trays and be sure there is a trash can close to the work table. When your child tells you she wants to do artwork, it will be easier for both of you. Once your child understands she is to stay in one place and follow your other rules, you will both be happier, she can have a wider range of art materials, and you will be more likely to encourage all her art activities.

CRAYONS—Your child may already have crayons, but if they are not the large or jumbo style, purchase a set. These crayons are made just for little hands.

PAPER—One of the cheapest ways to buy paper is by the ream (500 sheets). This may seem like a lot of paper, but I can almost guarantee your child will use all 500 sheets in one year. The paper should be large enough for your child to color easily—a good size is 12" x 18". A ream of 80 lb. white sulphite or manila paper is a good, inexpensive kind of paper for your child. The word "pound" is a term for a specific quality of paper and does not refer to the weight of the ream. Newsprint is another good source of drawing paper, but because it is so thin, I recommend buying it in 50-100 sheet pads to keep the paper neat and easy to use. Young children also love to draw on paper from a roll. The best type of paper for this is a 40-50 lb. kraft or banner paper. You can also use brown mailing paper.

PLAY CLAY — Your child will enjoy a container of play clay. This can be made or purchased under a variety of names. Let her create her own sculptures rather than purchasing the cookie cutter shapes many manufacturers sell with the product. This activity must have close supervision because the younger child may put it in her mouth or let some fall to the floor. Be sure the play clay is nontoxic.

Item	Size, Weight, Quantity
Sulphite drawing paper	12" x 18", 40-50 lb., 500 sheets
Roll of kraft or banner paper	36" x 25", 40-50 lb.
Newsprint tablet	12" x 18", 20-30 lb.
Jumbo crayons, large diameter	8-12 colors
Safety scissors with blunt tip, good quality	
White school glue	$4^1/2$ oz. and 16 oz. bottles
6 bars nontoxic, non-hardening clay: red, yellow, terra cotta, violet, white, turquoise	1 lb. bars

ART SUPPLIES FOR CHILDREN AGES 6 AND 7

The art supplies for this age are similar to those of the younger child, but as he develops more coordination, he can handle more sophisticated tools. Safety still has to be a priority. Sharp items like scissors and pencils should only be used while sitting at a table.

CRAYONS—The large, jumbo crayons are still a good choice, but you may want to try using the regular-sized crayons in a box of twelve to sixteen assorted colors. Encourage him to use the crayons that are broken by removing the paper so he can color using the flat side.

CRAYON STORAGE BOX—Keeping crayons in their original box can be very frustrating for a young child. A strong plastic box with a hinged lid (like a lunchbox) will help him keep them organized.

MARKERS—Kids love large washable markers. Purchase the fat kind with a large diameter. Bargain markers usually have washed-out looking colors and only a small amount of pigment in them. Purchase a good name brand for this first set of markers.

PENCIL—The best kind of pencil for drawing is a #2B. A child this age needs a pencil with a large diameter because his hand and finger muscles are usually not ready for the pencils that are common to adults. Stores sometimes refer to them as beginner's pencils. Another kind of pencil your child may enjoy using is a carpenter's pencil; it's a large, flat, wide pencil. A pencil can be dangerous to a young child if it is not used correctly. Be sure he understands that he is to sit in a chair or lie on the floor while using it and is never to throw it or put it in his mouth.

ERASER—The erasers at the end of pencils are usually so hard that they do not work well at removing pencil marks. The best erasers are the kinds he can hold in his hand, made of a soft pink rubber, soft gum, or plastic. The new plastic and vinyl erasers work well and even come in different shapes for young children. If possible, try the eraser before purchasing it or buy several different kinds to see which he prefers.

PENCIL SHARPENER — Hand-held pencil sharpeners are often better than the electric and mounted varieties. Purchase two or three because they tend to get lost. You may also want to get a sharpener in a container-style so the pencil shavings won't get on the floor.

GLUE—White school glue works well on most projects and is usually a good buy. Purchase your child's glue in a bottle no bigger than 4½ oz. and refill it when empty. If the nozzle gets clogged, soak it in warm soapy water for several hours, then push the old glue out with a toothpick, and repeat this until the hole in the nozzle is clear. Liquid roll-on glue can be used too. Paste is messy, comes out in clumps, and tends to get hard before you finish the jar.

SCISSORS—Great care must be taken when using scissors. Explain to your child he is to use them only at a table or while sitting on the floor. Purchase good, moderately priced, safety scissors with rounded tips until he is at least seven or eight.

PAPER—You might want to purchase drawing paper in bulk (by the ream) to save yourself a lot of money. (For the type of paper to buy, see the "Supplies for Children Ages 2 to 5.") Your child will also enjoy colored construction paper, a tablet of sulphite or newsprint drawing paper, and kraft or banner paper in a roll for making murals and large drawings.

FINGER PAINT—Kids love to finger paint, but the mess usually limits the number of times you will use it. Therapists sometimes use it to help people relax and to get in touch with the playful side of the personality. Many adults who were never given the chance to do finger painting as children feel they have missed something very important in their childhood. If you can, purchase a finger painting kit with paper in it. If you plan on letting your child use it more than once, or if you want to join in yourself, purchase the paint in pint jars of the following colors: yellow, blue, red, white, and purple (kids love purple and it's all but impossible to get a "pretty" purple by mixing the standard shades of red and blue). Finger paints need a slick surfaced paper. It is simply called finger painting paper. It normally comes in packages of 100 sheets.

TEMPERA PAINT—Tempera paint comes in liquid, powder, and cake form. Your child will probably find the cakes of tempera paint produce bright colors and are easy to set up and clean up. A set of eight colors is enough. Large cakes are preferable to the smaller ones at this age. Watercolor sets usually produce washed-out colors, the paint is difficult to control, and the pans of color are too small for the paint brushes.

PAINT BRUSHES—Your child will also need several large paint brushes. They come in sizes that are numbered 1, 2, 3, 4, or 5, etc. A #1 brush is smaller than a #2. Your child will most enjoy brushes in sizes 5 through 12. He will need watercolor brushes in round and flat styles. Purchase three round point and one flat. Avoid bargain brushes and get a good, moderately priced paint brush that will last many years. You can tell a good paint brush by gently pulling on the bristles. If some fall out and the bristles do not return to their original position, do not buy it. Buy good brushes, help him keep them clean, and they will last for many years. Some of my favorite paint brushes are more than twenty years old.

TAPE—He will also need his own roll of tape. Purchase a roll each of masking and removable transparent tape.

DRAWING TOOLS—A plastic, wood, or flexible acrylic ruler and plexiglass triangle are two basic drawing tools that all artists, young and old, should have in the studio.

CLAY—The non-hardening clays are great for kids who like to make sculptures. They come in a variety of colors and can be used over and over again. Be sure to get the nontoxic variety.

Item	Size, Weight, Quantity
Jumbo crayons	Set of 8
Sulphite drawing paper	80 lb., 500 sheets
Safety scissors with blunt tips	
White school glue	$4^1/2$ oz. and 16 oz. bottles
Masking tape	$3/4$"
Removable transparent tape	Small roll with dispenser
Jumbo tempera paint cubes	Set of 8 colors
Paint brushes	Sizes 6, 8, and 10
Floor model child's easel with one or two melamine boards (no chalkboards)	
4 large bulldog clips for easel	
2 beginner's pencils	Size 2B
Soft gum and vinyl erasers	
Finger paints: red, yellow, blue, purple, and white	4 oz. jars
Finger paint paper	12" x 18"
Hand-held pencil sharpener with container	
Medium-sized plexiglass triangle	
Package of assorted colored paper	
Nontoxic modeling clay, non-hardening variety: red, terra	

cotta, white, turquoise, yellow, violet, light green	1 lb. bars
Banner or kraft paper	36" x 25', 40-50 lb.

Extra Supplies for Children Ages 6 and 7

Gummed colored paper—just moisten the paper and it sticks, comes in precut shapes or sheets

Old wallpaper books

Paper assortment—some catalogs offer an assortment of papers like cellophane, tissue, metallic, colored, crepe

Sketch pads—50 sheets of sulphite paper or kraft paper

Blank greeting cards and envelopes

Brass paper fasteners

Paper punch

Loop weaving set—purchase the 7³/₄" size loom (smaller size makes a potholder that is too small) and a 4 oz. or 1 lb. bag of loops

Wiggle eyes that can be glued on paper

Plastic or wood beads with a hole large enough to push thread through easily without a needle

Thread for stringing beads—waxed nylon twine or dental floss

ART SUPPLIES FOR CHILDREN
AGES 8 AND 9

The art supplies for this age are about the same as for the five to seven year old. You may want to add some new items because your child will now be more safety conscious, and her small muscle coordination allows for handling smaller items with greater ease. Safety still must be a priority. Sharp items like scissors and pencils should only be used while sitting at a table.

CRAYONS—Your child will still enjoy crayons, but will prefer the crayons with a larger selection of colors. She will especially enjoy a large box of sixty-four crayons. An extra storage box for these crayons will help keep the ones that are broken from getting lost in the original box. Purchase crayons from established companies or buy the name brand of a catalog supply company.

PENCILS—Regular pencils are not suitable for drawing because they are usually too hard. Purchase a #2B drawing pencil. If your child tends to lend out her pencils, you might get a turquoise drawing pencil. These are excellent pencils and such an unusual color that your child is less likely to have them returned.

ERASER — Purchase a gum, vinyl, or soft rubber eraser. Erasers at the ends of pencils are usually too hard to do a good job erasing pencil marks.

SCISSORS—Your child will now want a better pair of scissors than the safety scissors. You might consider purchasing a pair of stainless steel scissors with a safety rounded tip. They cut well and come in a variety of sizes. If possible, let her try cutting with several of the smaller sizes to see what feels comfortable.

RULER—A ruler and a clear plastic triangle are needed.

GLUE — White school glue, roll-on glue, and glue sticks all work well.

PAINT — Large cubes of tempera paint in sets of 8-10 colors are still a good buy.

WATERCOLOR BRUSHES—Purchase good quality brushes in sizes 10, 6, 5, 3, and 1. She might also enjoy sponge brushes. Inexpensive brushes are a waste of money and can be very frustrating to a young artist. I also recommend that you clean the brushes once in a while. Children really do not understand the importance of getting every speck of paint out of the bristles. Dry brushes in a horizontal position.

You might consider getting a special case for brushes or a special paint brush cleaning tub to keep her brushes in good condition so they will last longer.

PAPER—Purchase white sulphite or manila paper in reams. A good, inexpensive source of paper is computer or copy paper. She will also enjoy colored construction paper and rolls of kraft paper for murals.

MARKERS—Purchase name-brand watercolor markers, or an art catalog's house brand, with medium to wide felt tips.

EASEL — The old-fashioned kindergarten easel is still very popular. Purchase one with a melamine surface. This is a white, slick surface that can be drawn on with crayons and dry erase markers. Get large bulldog clips to hold the paper to the easel while painting.

TAPE—She will need a roll of masking tape and a roll of removable transparent tape for some projects and to hang up artwork.

CLAY—The non-hardening clays are great for kids who like to make sculptures. They come in a variety of colors and can be used over and over again. If she would prefer to keep her clay sculptures, you can also find clay that can be baked in the oven until hard and then painted.

Item	Size, Weight, Quantity
Crayons	Set of 64
Storage box for crayons	
Turquoise drawing pencils	2B, 3
Soft pink eraser	
Hand-held container-style pencil sharpener	
White sulphite drawing paper	12" x 18", 500 sheets
White school glue	$4^1/_2$ oz. and 16 oz. bottles
Plastic ruler	
Acrylic triangle—medium	
Removable transparent tape	
Masking tape	$^3/_4$"
Tempera paint	Set of 12 cakes or liquid in bottles
Watercolor paint brushes	#10, 6, 5, 3, 1
Storage box for paint brushes	
Markers	Set of 12
Stainless steel scissors	4" and 7"
Painting easel or adjustable-height drafting table	

Extra Supplies for Children Ages 8 and 9

Postcards

Beginning art or drawing books

Large lettering stencils

Small burlap squares for stitching yarn designs

Pompons, craft fur, and felt scraps

Pipe cleaners or chenille stems—the jumbo stems work better for small hands

Corks—box of 50 in various sizes

Glitter glue

Sidewalk chalk

Sequins

Wood variety package—scraps of various sizes and shapes

Paper assortment (see previous section)

Sketch pads

Blank greeting cards

ART SUPPLIES FOR CHILDREN
AGES 10 AND 11

A child at this age will still enjoy the art materials listed for the eight and nine year old but will now be able to handle more complex materials. This is a good age to let children try crafts, sculpture, and even photography. This is an exciting time for your child, because he now has enough skill and patience to try a variety of good art materials.

PAPER—Buy white sulphite paper, 12" x 18", 50 lb. weight. You can also purchase computer paper, copy paper, oatmeal paper (a textured light brown drawing paper), paper in a roll, colored paper, and fadeless construction paper. Kids at this age, for some reason, use a lot of black, so you might get an extra package. Look for assorted paper packs in catalogs.

COLORED PENCILS—Your child may be tired of crayons and may want to experiment with other coloring media like colored pencils. Purchase a good, moderately priced set of as many colors as you can afford. Avoid the cheap varieties because the price usually indicates the manufacturer put more clay and less pigment into the colors. A small set of quality colored pencils is better than a large set of the bargain variety.

You can also purchase colored pencils that turn into watercolors when used with a wet paint brush. Charcoal colored pencils are also available. Be careful to order the kind you want when ordering from a catalog. I didn't read my catalog closely one year and purchased charcoal colored pencils instead of the regular variety. They were beautiful pencils, but I do not like charcoal; it is too messy, it smears, and you have to spray it with fixative when you are done. They're best for those who especially like to use black charcoal pencils.

PENCILS—Drawing pencils, for the most part, need to be soft. Purchase #2B, 3B, or 4B. He may also enjoy a flat sketching #4B pencil, a white pencil, and a black charcoal pencil.

ERASER—Gum erasers are kneaded into a soft, pliable ball, which when rubbed against a pencil mark erases it almost completely. They are especially good with charcoal pencils. There are also soft rubber and vinyl erasers that remove pencil marks easily. Try erasers before purchasing if possible.

PENCIL SHARPENERS — Buy hand-held, container-style

sharpeners.

MARKERS—Markers come in sets of 10 to 60 different colors. Some companies offer fluorescent and metallic colors. Your child will enjoy using different tips. Markers are available in extra wide, chisel, bold, regular, fine, and brush tips.

GLUE—Purchase white school glue, glue sticks, or roll-on glue. If your child likes sculpting, you will also need a stronger glue that is made to adhere to nonporous materials. These can be dangerous to use, so be sure to purchase the nontoxic variety. If he will be gluing wood, get wood glue. Never let glue freeze.

TAPE—Buy masking, removable transparent, and double-stick tape.

SCISSORS—Stainless steel scissors, 5" long, are a good choice. Still stress the safety precautions involved in using scissors. For detailed cutting, get an extra small pair. Hand-held sharpeners are available. If he is working on sculptures, you may want to get a pair of wire snips, so he won't be tempted to cut things other than paper with his scissors.

PAINTS—If your child wants to try something new, he can try watercolors. Be sure to purchase a quality set at a moderate price, not a bargain brand. Good watercolor paints will last a long time, the colors are stronger, and the paint dissolves quickly onto the brush.

He can use his watercolors on sulphite paper but will find they work better on watercolor paper. A good kind for beginners is the 90 lb. paper. Watercolor paper is expensive, but the sheets are usually very large and can be cut into smaller pieces. Most watercolor paper can be used on front and back.

Your child might also enjoy a set of acrylic paints. They come in jars or tubes and clean up with water. He can use them on paper, canvas, wood, clay, and even metal.

WATERCOLOR BRUSHES—Purchase good quality brushes in a variety of sizes—#10, 6, 5, 3, and 1. To keep them in good condition, get a case for the brushes or a paint brush cleaning tub to hold the brushes upright. After the brushes have been thoroughly cleaned, the bristles should be reshaped to their original position and dried horizontally.

YARN—Yarn can be purchased for local craft stores or from some art catalogs. If he wants to weave, he also needs a loom, a long plastic weaving needle, and some warp thread.

If your child wants to do stitchery, he will need cloth, short metal or plastic needles with a large eye, and a good variety of yarns. Yarn paintings need yarn, glue, a piece of heavy cardboard or wood, and toothpicks. Some good materials to do stitchery work on are burlap and monk's, Aida, or canvas cloth. He may also want to try making rugs, knitting, crocheting, or quilt making.

SCULPTURE—Non-hardening clay is still a good choice, but he may prefer a modeling compound that is more permanent. Some varieties cure or harden in the oven. He may also enjoy a set of clay modeling tools. My students enjoy a clay gun. It is an inexpensive tool that produces a variety of clay strands that can be added to sculptures for unusual effects.

Working on sculptures is very difficult without some sort of turntable that spins the sculpture around so he can work on all sides without lifting it off the table.

Other modeling materials he may enjoy are soapstone, plaster, and soft wood. Each requires different modeling tools.

DRAWING TOOLS—He will need a T-square, a ruler, and a clear acrylic triangle.

Item	Size, Weight, Quantity
Modeling clay, self-hardening	2-lb. pkg.
Quality watercolors, moderate price	Set of 12
Round watercolor brushes	#10, 6, 5, 3, 1
Plastic tub for holding and cleaning brushes	
Bag of assorted yarn remnants	5 lb.
Chipboard weaving loom	$9^3/4$" x 13"
3 plastic weaving needles	2 6" and 1 3"
Sulphite drawing paper	12" x 18", 500 sheets
Oatmeal drawing pad	12" x 18", 50 sheets
Watercolor paper	18" x 24", 90 lb.
Fadeless art paper	12" x 18", 30 sheets
Stainless steel scissors	5" and 8"
Wire snips	
Masking tape	$3/4$"
Removable transparent tape	
Markers, chisel-tipped, waterbased ink	Set of 12
Markers, fine-tipped, waterbased ink	Set of 30
Turquoise drawing pencils	#HB, 2B, and 6B
Flat-lead sketching pencil	#4B

White charcoal pencil
Watercolor pencils   Set of 12
Hand-held container-style pencil
    sharpener
T-square, wood with plastic or metal
    edge
Clear acrylic triangle   Medium
Ruler, flexible metal   12"
Erasers, gum and vinyl

Extra Supplies for Children Ages 10 and 11

Fan-style paint brush
Rotary tray to hold paint brushes, pencils, erasers, etc.
Tool box to carry art supplies
Package of assorted papers
Pocket sketchbook
Poster board
Black sketching pens, permanent and waterbased
Inexpensive drafting table brush with 2-inch soft hair — to keep
    table clean and clear of debris
Compass and protractor
Two-harness or inkle weaving loom
Needlepoint canvas, 6 squares per inch
Felt, 9" x 12" pieces, or package of remnants
Fabric crayons, markers, or paint sets
Simple kits to introduce various crafts
Jewelry-making kit
Beads
Origami paper
Small manicure scissors for very detailed cutting
Starter set of chalk pastels

ART SUPPLIES FOR CHILDREN
AGES 12 AND 13

Children at this age are usually going through a lot of growth, which puts a strain on them physically as well as psychologically. Some of the children who were so obviously talented in art when they were younger may quit doing their artwork altogether. Talented kids, however, are usually so revered by their peers that it is hard for them to allow a budding artist to fade away completely. Mike, a fifth grader, needed a poster for a science fair project about the destruction of the rain forest. He tried and tried to draw the trees, without much success. His friend suggested that Lyn could help him. Mike asked her, but she said she didn't do art anymore. A big hush came over the room and somebody said, "Did you hear that? Lyn isn't going to draw anymore." What her teacher and I had been trying to get her to do for months was resolved in ten seconds. Lyn felt bad that she had let down not only her friend but her classmates too. She decided to draw just one more time. If your child is experiencing a "fallow" period as Lyn did, you can wait it out, try helping by asking for her help on a family project that requires artistic skills, get her an art-related book to read, or purchase new art supplies. Just as some of my students' interest in art was fading, I also found that a new interest in art was budding in other students.

Whether your child is just beginning to show an interest in art or always has, she cannot develop to full potential without proper materials. Some people feel that if you just give an artist paper and pencils it will be enough, but please consider purchasing some of the other supplies listed below. The basic supplies listed below will last well over a year. If your child is wasteful or unappreciative, you may want to start an art budget or have her share the cost of new art supplies.

PAPER—Buy sulphite paper as recommended in earlier sections. Your child will also enjoy her own spiral-bound sketchbook. Purchase 80 lb. watercolor paper if your child wants to watercolor.

Although buying good paper can be a strain on your budget, high quality paper will help your child learn to be extra careful with each piece of artwork. There's a story about a famous children's book illustrator whose entrepreneurial father gave his kids beautiful, high quality paper for their artwork. Every time one of his businesses failed, which was at least once a year, he would give all his expensive (and now useless to him) business stationery to his children. They loved getting the paper and thanked him by creating beautiful pictures. Not all his children became artists, but one did become a famous illustrator.

Your child will also need poster board, an array of good quality, non-fading colored papers, and a package of black or dark gray paper.

PAINTS—Buy a set of moderately priced watercolors. The tempera paints she used when she was younger may still be satisfactory, but if you can afford it, purchase a set of acrylic paints. This paint comes in tubes or jars and is a lot like oil paint except that it requires only water to thin it and clean the brushes. The paint will stain, so care must be used when working with it. An inexpensive set will be fine. She will need ten basic colors: black, white, burnt umber (dull dark brown), raw umber (light reddish brown), yellow ochre, light or scarlet red, cobalt blue, light green, dioxazine purple, and ultramarine blue.

Another item that will help her learn about painting and using color is a color wheel poster. Basic information about mixing and using colors is on it. Until she works with color for several years this is an invaluable tool.

She will also need an enamel tray on which to mix paints. Wax paper or a heavy piece of plastic can also be used. Acrylic paints work well on heavy paper, poster board, canvas, fabric, plastic, metal, and wood.

PAINT BRUSHES—Watercolor brushes, for the most part, have pointed tips and are softer than oil and acrylic brushes. If you can, purchase a set of each kind. Paint brushes in the moderate price range are your best buy; the inexpensive ones lose their bristles and do not hold a point. A place to store brushes is important; brushes stored improperly can be rendered useless in a matter of months. Your child might also enjoy a bamboo paint brush and several foam paint brushes.

SCISSORS—See previous section.

ADHESIVES — Sobo™ glue is a good alternative to white school glue, but regular school glue is still a good choice. She may also want to use tacky glue, bond glue, and stick glues. To glue metals or nonporous surfaces, she will need an adhesive that is nontoxic, sniff proof, and nonflammable. Name brands are usually your best buy.

PENCIL SHARPENER—See previous section.

COLORED PENCILS—A large set of good colored pencils is one of the best gifts you can give your child. There are several varieties: regular soft leaded, erasable, watercolor, and pastel colored pencils. I only recommend the regular pencils and the watercolor. Quality pencil sets are worth the money because they produce the brightest colors, last longer, and allow you to replace individual colors. Art stores also offer pencil lengtheners. These allow your child to use the pencil down to the very last inch.

PASTELS — Pastels are a soft, powdery, easily blendable medium, sometimes referred to as chalk, that your child may especially enjoy because they are so different from other coloring media. Pastels can be blended with the fingers, a soft cloth, or you can purchase some inexpensive blending tools. Pastels require special paper, and the final project has to be sealed with a fixative to keep it from smearing. I suggest that you purchase a liquid fixative and put it in a safety spray bottle. If you can only find it in aerosol spray form, use it outside. Pastels can be used on kraft or charcoal paper or any paper that has a slight tooth (texture) to it. Your child may also enjoy a new kind of pastel on the market that crumbles less, blends better, and is stronger than regular pastels or chalks.

PENCILS — Pencils with soft lead or graphite are good for drawing. You can buy a set of drawing pencils or purchase them individually. She should have at least one 2B pencil. A good set of drawing pencils with different degrees of softness (HB, B, 2B, 3B, 4B, 5B, and 6B) will make it easier to create shadows and will give him a broad range of the black shades. She might also enjoy a 2B black charcoal pencil, a white charcoal pencil, and a graphite, water-soluble pencil.

ERASER—Gum and rubber pencil erasers need to be soft so they will not damage the paper. Erasers also come in plastic and vinyl.

TAPE—Masking tape 3/4" or larger will come in handy, as will removable transparent tape and double-stick transparent tape.

MARKERS — A good combination of broad, medium, and fine tipped watercolor markers in a wide array of colors will provide endless hours of enjoyment for your child. Some marker products that she will enjoy include metallic colors, fluorescent colors, brush tip markers, markers that are permanent on any surface, and fabric markers. Purchase a moderately priced good name brand or the house brand of a large art store.

RULERS—She will need a good T-square, a clear acrylic triangle, a measured ruler, a compass, and stencil letter guides. Although hand lettering is a better choice, sometimes lettering stencils are preferred. The paper variety is inexpensive and comes in a wide range of lettering styles.

CLAY—Your child can make beautiful sculptures with non-hardening or self-hardening clays, papier maché, plaster, soft stone, wire, and wood. A small revolving stand or turntable will give easy access to all sides of the sculpture. She will also need a few carving and sculpting tools.

YARN—Weaving, stitchery, knitting, crochet, and soft sculpture all use yarn. Weaving is especially popular with this age group. Looms are very expensive and hard to set up, so for her first weavings, purchase an inexpensive cardboard loom. They are easy to set up and use and can be carried just about anywhere. To make a weaving, she will also need warp thread and a long needle with a large eye. A wide variety of yarns will help her be more creative in her projects. Remnant yarn can be purchased by the pound inexpensively from large catalog companies. It comes in a wide variety of colors and textures. There are many books for beginners on each of the above crafts.

Item	Size, Weight, Quantity
Sketch pad	30 sheets
White sulphite paper	12" x 18", 70 lb., 500 sheets
Spiral white sulphite drawing tablet	
Kraft paper drawing tablet	50 sheets
Watercolor sketch pad	90 lb., 12 sheets
Poster board, 4-ply, buff colored	22" x 28"
Black construction paper	12" x 18", 50 sheets
Fadeless colored art paper	18" x 24", 60 sheets
Jars of acrylic paints	Set of 6 2 oz. jars
Set of oil and acrylic paint brushes	6
Watercolor brushes	Sizes 00, 2, 4, 6, and a $1/4$" oval mop brush
Wash tub and paint brush holder	
Foam paint brushes	1", 2", and 3"
Bamboo paint brush	#1
Canvas boards, primed	1 5" x 7" and 2 9" x 12"
Stainless steel scissors	$5^1/2$" and $7^1/2$"
All-purpose utility snips	7"
White glue	$4^1/2$ oz. and 16 oz. bottles
Tacky glue	6 oz.
Multi-purpose glue	
Colored pencils	Set of 48
Pencil lengthener	
Set of pastels	
White charcoal paper	11" x 17" pad
Pastel brush set	

Package medium blending stumps	12
Turquoise drawing pencils	HB, B, 2B, 3B, 5B, 6B
Charcoal pencils, black and white	2B
Kneadable eraser	
Soft gum eraser	
Masking tape	$^3/_4$"
Transparent tape—removable and double-stick	
Watercolor markers, fine point	Set of 12
Chisel-tipped fluorescent markers	6
Brush-tip markers	Set of 6
Black watercolor markers, fine, regular, and bold	
T-square, wood with metal edge	
Triangle, acrylic	10"
Compass	
Paper stencil lettering guides, Roman style	$^3/_4$" and 2"
Storage box with handle	
Yarns, earth tones	5 oz. cones, set of 16
Weaving needles	6", 3
Chipboard looms	$9^3/_4$" x 13", 2

Extra Supplies for Children Ages 12 and 13

Bracelet, barrette, earring forms
Origami paper
Blank greeting cards
Crepe paper
Tissue paper
Blank postcards
Lettering stencils
Sequins, beads, feathers
Drawing clipboard
Foil paper
Cellophane paper

Camera
Computer graphics program
Foam blocks
Soft carving blocks
Craft wire
Variety of stitchery cloth and threads
Felt, small squares
Craft Popsicle sticks
Wood plaques
Textile paints
Carving tools

ART SUPPLIES FOR CHILDREN
AGES 14 THROUGH 18

Your high school-aged child may have been developing his skills since he was a young child, or he may be just beginning to study art.

The supplies needed for a more advanced student are presented in this section. If your child has just begun an interest in art, the supplies listed for the twelve to fourteen year old will be fine for the first year. Because he is older, he will probably learn the art skills quickly and be ready for the advanced art supplies listed in this section after the second year studying art.

Not mentioned in this section, but of great importance when studying a specific medium, are books on each subject. Your child will greatly benefit from reading books that explain how to use a specific medium. Most schools do not spend a lot of money on art books, so check with the reference librarian in your public library. What she doesn't have, she can probably obtain through inter-library loan. It is also a good idea to purchase a few books and a subscription to an art magazine for your child's own library.

Art classes in high school or with a private tutor are usually in one specific art area and require special supplies. Your child might take a course in painting, photography, or print making. Art materials for each class will be different; therefore, supplies recommended in this section are listed by area of art instruction.

Painting (Oil or Acrylic)

In a painting class your child will be asked to purchase a set of oil or acrylic paints. I chose acrylics when I was in school because I do not like the smell of oil paints or the turpentine used to clean the brushes. Some artists, like my mother, feel that there is no other paint than oils. If your child is being tutored, his teacher may insist on oil paints, so check with him before you make your purchase. For your sake and that of all the members of your family, I suggest that your child use only acrylics.

Your child will also need something to paint on. Many teachers begin their students on Masonite boards or canvas panels. The more advanced students use canvas, stretched and secured onto a wood frame. To keep the paint from absorbing into the board or canvas, it needs to be covered with a primer. The most common primer used by painters is made of plaster of Paris and glue, and is called *gesso*.

Acrylic paint comes in jars or tubes; oil paint mainly in tubes. The two kinds of paint are not compatible, so your child cannot use them together on the same painting. Acrylic paints come in more than seventy colors, but a basic set of twelve is enough to get started. As you help your child choose the colors of paint, you will find many have unusual color names. Here are the basic colors, without the fancy names, that I have in my art box: a large 8 oz. tube of white and 2 oz. tubes of jet black, bluish purple, light yellow, crimson (purplish red), scarlet (bright red with a touch of orange), yellow-orange, emerald green, phthalocyanine blue (dark blue) ultramarine blue (light blue), burnt umber (dark brown), and burnt sienna (reddish brown). An inexpensive brand of acrylics is fine for the first year of painting; then you can purchase a moderately priced brand.

Good paint brushes are a necessity as your child begins to work with acrylics and oils. Oil paint brushes are usually made of sable (the tail fur of a weasel-like animal), and acrylic brushes are usually made of white nylon (erminette or taklon). Paint brushes come in a variety of sizes and shapes. A good selection for a young artist might include round brushes in sizes 0, 2, and 4 and flat in sizes 2, 4, and 6. She might also enjoy a fan brush, a bristle brush, and a palette knife.

Acrylics have a companion product called *gel medium*. This is designed to help the artist make acrylic paints cover a larger area, increase the time they can be used before they dry, and help get a thick, textured effect in paintings. The final painting will need a coat of varnish to protect it. For acrylics you can use a matte (non-glare satin finish) or gloss medium as a varnish; for oils, use a damar varnish. If you are using oil paints, purchase brush cleaner or turpentine for cleaning up your tools. When purchasing turpentine for your child, be sure to keep this story about my first painting class in mind. While attending a summer painting class at Northwestern University, I found out the hard way that there really are two kinds of turpentine. When I opened my can of turpentine to clean off my paint brush, I was immediately made aware of my mistake by every-one in the class. The smell was so bad that my fellow students ran to the windows and opened them as wide as possible. Everyone was asking who did it, and my red face gave me away. With self-preser-vation on everyone's mind, all the oil painters in the class offered to lend me their low odor variety. I took the cheap, smelly turpentine home to my dad's workshop, gave my mom the oil paints, and bought all acrylic paints. My classmates thanked me, the skin on my hands thanked me, and my paint brushes were much cleaner be-cause I didn't mind cleaning them.

Your teen also needs a tray to put his paints on—a palette. A covered palette will keep the paint moist until the next time he uses it. Acrylics work well on a porcelain butcher's tray because the paints don't adhere. These are expensive, but this kind of tray lasts almost forever; mine is going on twenty-two years old. Oil painters usually prefer a wood or plastic palette.

A floor easel is very nice to have but until he is serious about his artwork, you may want just to provide a table easel. The most important aspect of either a table or a full standing easel is that it must be sturdy. Any collapsible easel should have a locking device on the legs to hold them in place. He will be pushing with the paint brush on all corners of the painting surface, so he will need a very sturdy easel. Painting on a flat table is almost impossible; it is hard on your neck and upper back to work in this position for a long time. Your teen will enjoy an easel because he can then stand back from the work and see how it looks from a distance.

The final item he will need is a box in which to keep painting supplies. Many students use a steel tool box. They are inexpensive, easy to carry, and last a long time. In one high school, carrying an art tool box was considered a status symbol. The art students were so revered by their classmates because of their active participation in advertising the school and all of its activities that it was a status symbol to carry an art box.

Selecting the right supplies from an art store or a catalog can be confusing, so I have included a list of supplies that your teen will need if he wants to paint.

Item	Size, Weight, Quantity
Primed canvas panels	9" x 12", 3
Primed canvas panels	18" x 24", 2
Acrylic titanium white paint	8 oz. tube
Acrylic paint (inexpensive brand): black, violet, light yellow, crimson, scarlet red, yellow-orange, phthalocyanine blue, ultramaine blue, phthalo green, burnt sienna, raw umber, yellow ochre	2 oz. tube of each color
Gesso	1 quart
Acrylic gel medium, matte	1 pint
Matte varnish	1 pint
Round nylon erminette or taklon acrylic brushes	Sizes 0, 2, 4

Flat nylon erminette or taklon acrylic brushes	Sizes 2, 4, 6
Bristle fan brush	Size 2
Bristle brush	1"
Long palette knife with straight offset blade	
Paint saver palette with cover and moisture retainer	
Steel paint and brush box	
Auto-lock aluminum table easel	20" x 24"
Steel tool box with handle	
Brush washer with spiral brush holder/rack	

Watercolor Painting

Watercolor paints should be purchased in the moderately priced sets of twelve different colored cakes and a .47 fl. oz. tube of white. If your teen has worked in watercolors for a while, he may enjoy having all his paint in tube form. He will also need paint brushes. Professional watercolorist Edgar A. Whitney, in his book *The Complete Guide to Watercolor Painting*, recommends red sable round brushes in sizes 14, 10, 6, 3, and 2 and a 1" red sable flat. If you can find a 2" camel hair flat brush, it will also come in handy. The best paper is 140 lb. all-rag. A piece of Masonite can be used as a drawing board. Put a block of 2" x 2" wood under it to place the board at a slight angle.

Item	Size, Weight, Quantity
Watercolors, cake	Set of 12
White tube watercolor	.47 fluid oz.
Brushes, red sable round	Sizes 14, 10, 6, 3, 2
Brush, red sable flat	1"
All-rag paper	140 lb., 10" x 14", 10 sheets
Masonite panel	18" x 24"
Bulldog paper clips	3", 4
Small sponge	
Pencil	2B
Covered watercolor palette	
Paint box for brushes and paints	
Single-edge razor blades	Box of 5
Masking tape	1"

Sculpture or Three-Dimensional Art

Sculpture can be done in a variety of media. The most common is clay. Clay requires a kiln to finish the drying process. If your young artist wants to work on sculptures at home, he can use a clay that hardens in the oven or one that is self-hardening. Professional sculptors use a non-hardening material called modeling clay. It has many unique qualities that make it a good medium for your child to use at home.

Papier maché is another form of sculpture. The old method of glue and strips of paper has been improved with a product called Sculptamold. Large sculptures are usually placed over a wire armature, and when the papier maché is dry, you can saw, carve, or even sand it.

Sculpture can also be created by using wire, wax, and found materials (branches, metal scraps, shells ...). If he would like to try carving stone without using chisels and sculpture tools, he can try soapstone or sandstone. A good set of carving tools is necessary only after he has chosen the carving material he likes best. Until that time, he can improvise with tools found around the house. Be sure he has a small revolving table to help see the work from all sides without moving it.

Books are an invaluable asset to the new sculptor. There is a beginner's book on almost every sculpture material available. New products on the market give complete instructions on how to use the material when you purchase it.

Item	Size, Weight, Quantity
Styling clay, red-brown, non-hardening	2 lb. pkg.
Styling wax	1 lb. pkg.
Efaplast modeling material, white	500 grams
FIMO modeling material	Set of 15, 1 oz. each
Wood modeling tools	Set of 5
Sculptor's steel modeling tools	Set of 4
Turntable	

Sculptures can also be made out of wood. He can whittle on an old chunk of wood and learn it himself, but it would probably be better if he learned it from a professional, by watching a video, or by reading a book about carving wood. Carving on wood should only be done with the proper tools. Your teen might also enjoy making model buildings. Architects make their house models out of a lightweight wood called balsa. You can order it in thin strips in a wide range of lengths and widths. The balsa wood is easily cut with a utility knife, secured with wood glue or a glue gun, and then stained or painted. Model buildings can also be made with cardboard.

Sculptures can also be made out of scraps of old discarded items. Indianapolis has a beautiful fountain made of old discarded musical instruments. If your teen likes to make this type of sculpture, he will need a good all-purpose adhesive. Hot melt glue guns work well, and so do the clear adhesives that secure non-porous materials. Care needs to be taken with either product. Please talk to your child about these products before allowing him to use them.

Item	Size, Weight, Quantity
Wood blocks of varying hardness	Approximately 3" x 3" x 8", 3
Wood carving tool set	
Soft carving brick	$2^1/_2$" x $4^1/_2$" x 9"
E-Z Karv plastic foam blocks	3" x 3" x 8"
Soapstone	4 lbs.
Steel sculpting tools	Set of 6
Balsa wood scrap bag	24 pieces, 5
Wood glue	8 oz.
Utility or art knife	
Extra blades for utility knife	Pkg. of 5 or 6
Sandpaper and steel wool	Varying grades

Print Making

Print making is done in a variety of ways. The most common for a beginner is carving into a linoleum or wood block. To do this properly, he will need linoleum-cutting or wood-carving tools. Once the block is cut or carved it needs to be inked and pressed onto paper. At school he will use a special printing press to make a print. At home he can simply put the ink on the carved surface with a brayer and then press it onto the paper. He might enjoy kits put out by Hunt-Speedball that give all the materials necessary to produce greeting cards, banners, small posters, etc. Other forms of print making he might enjoy are cutting stencils, silkscreen, etching, engraving, and rubber stamps.

Item	Size/Weight/Quantity
Linoleum blocks	3" x 4", 4" x 5", and 5" x 7"
Linoleum cutters, assorted	Set of 6 blades
Linoleum cutter handles	2
Brayer (hard)	4"
Waterbase black printing ink	37cc tube
Speedball Printmasters paper	9" x 12", 100 sheets
Greeting card kit	

Drawing

Supplies for a drawing class seem to be quite simple—pencils and paper. However, if you consider all the different kinds of paper and the different drawing materials, there is an exciting range of materials you can purchase for a class in drawing. Newsprint, computer paper, and copy paper are the least expensive kinds of paper you can purchase. Newsprint should be purchased in the 35 lb. weight. This is sketching paper and is used by artists who need to make quick drawings that will more than likely be thrown away. Your child may, however, want to spend a great deal of time on each drawing. You can purchase a pad of 90 lb. drawing paper. A drawing pad will give him the opportunity to observe this progress. The spiral-bound type is easiest to use. Other kinds of paper he may enjoy are: graph paper, tracing paper (vellum), blank greeting cards, a roll of kraft paper, several sheets of illustration board—one cold press (slightly textured) and one hot press (smooth), and 100% cotton charcoal paper with a slightly raised texture.

Drawing can be done with any number of tools from pencils to markers. Most people prefer pencils. Drawing pencils usually are soft graphite and are labeled B, 1B, 2B, 3B, 4B, 5B, 6B, 7B, 8B, and 9B. They can be purchased in a set or individually. He may also enjoy the following types of pencils: an oval sketch, a 6B charcoal, a carbon, a graphite, and a lead holder.

Purchase a pencil sharpener that he can carry easily and that holds the shavings. Some artists prefer to sharpen pencils with a knife and use a sandpaper pad to get the pencil just the way they want it. He will also need an eraser, and will probably enjoy several kinds: kneaded, gum, and vinyl. Manufacturers have also come up with an electric eraser. My architect friend Andy has one that removes the pencil marks so quickly and thoroughly, I wanted one too. When I asked him how much it cost, he said I didn't want to know. Let's just say it's over 100 times as expensive as the do-it-yourself variety. Erasures can make an awful mess on the paper and the drawing table, so you might also consider getting a dusting brush. These have a thin row of about 10" of horse or synthetic soft hair that he can brush over any surface to clean it without disturbing his drawing.

Colored pencils and crayons are also considered drawing tools. When purchasing colored pencils, be sure to buy the kind that have thick, soft lead. They are not cheap, but if you purchase a good set that can be supplemented each time a color is used up, you will find it a good buy overall. Some manufacturers offer over eighty different colors. Colored pencils come in regular soft lead, charcoal, and watercolor. All three are interesting, but most artists prefer the regular soft lead variety. Purchase as wide a range of colors as possible.

Charcoal is a popular drawing medium. It comes in three grades—soft, medium, and hard—and in several different forms: pencils, thin sticks, and thick rectangular sticks. Your child may like using charcoal because it's easy to erase and to create tonal gradations or shading. The best eraser to use with charcoal is the kneaded eraser. It is at its best when used on a paper with a heavy tooth or special charcoal paper and must be sprayed with a fixative when completed.

Crayon is actually the French word for pencil and has been used by young artists for well over a hundred years. However, crayons should not be left just to the young. Today we have them in water-soluble form, square sticks, over eighty different colors, and in a wax-oil form, similar to oil pastels.

Chalks and pastels are also drawing media. A pastel is softer than chalk and therefore can come in a wider and more brilliant range of color. Soft pastels come in over 250 different colors. The new "half-hard" pastels are cleaner and easier to use, but only come in ninety-six different colors. Blending stumps and small chamois are used to blend and shade with pastels. As with charcoal, pastels require fixative to secure the chalks to the paper.

Drawing is best done at a table or an easel that will hold the work in an almost upright position. He also needs a T-square, drafting tape (it will not tear paper when removed), and a few large bulldog clips to hold the paper to the board. Other tools that will help with drawing are an 18" transparent ruler, a clear plastic triangle, a French curve, a protractor, a compass, and a container for all these drawing supplies.

Markers are also considered drawing tools. The most expensive markers are best left to the professionals. You can, however, purchase a good set at a moderate price. Most drawing with markers is done with black ink. Water-soluble ink can be made into a wash by adding water to the ink on the paper. Permanent black ink creates a darker black and is best to use if the drawing is to be preserved or photocopied. Markers also come in a variety of tips. Ink drawings can also be done with a bottle of ink and a metal nib, a technical pen, or a fountain pen. Non-reproducing (also called non-photo or non-repro) pencils and pens will not reproduce on a copy machine or in the photographic process used by printers. An artist can sketch his idea with this pencil and then ink over it without ruining the final product. He can even write notes for the printer right on his drawing. Be sure he has at least one non-repro blue pencil.

Item	Size, Weight, Quantity
Newsprint pad	18" x 24", 35 lb., 100 sheets
White drawing paper	18"" x 24", 70 lb., 100 sheets
Drawing pad, fine tooth, spiral-bound	11" x 14", 50 lb., 100 sheets
Tracing vellum pad	11" x 14", 16 lb., 50 sheets
Greeting cards, white	Set of 20
Charcoal drawing pad	12" x 18", 24 sheets
Drawing pencils	Sizes H, 2B, 4B, 5B, 6B
Charcoal pencil	Size 2B
Drafting tape	
Tortillons and stumps for blending	12
Chamois, small	
Horsehair dusting brush	
Erasers, kneadable, gum, and plastic	
Pencil lengthener	
Container-style pencil sharpener	
Non-reproducing blue pencil	
Sandpaper pad	
Colored pencils	Set of 48
Spray fixative	$4^3/4$ oz.
Pastel starter kit	
T-square with plastic edge	
Plastic triangles	8" (45°,90°) and 12" (30°, 60°)
Clear plastic French curve	#10
Clear plastic protractor	8"
Flexible metal ruler	16"

Compass
Lettering template, block standard,
    $^5/_8$" bold
Slanted drawing table   Top measures 24" x 36"
Water-soluble black ink markers with
    tips: brush, fine, bullet, wedge,
    flat calligraphy
Fountain pen/India ink drawing set
Crow Quill Card drawing pen
    point & holder   12
Two-tiered storage box   14" x 7" x 5"

Crafts

The two terms "arts" and "crafts" are often used together. According to Rosalind Ragans' book, *Art Talk*, the definition of arts is, "... use of skill and imagination to produce beautiful objects." A craft is "... creating works of art that are both beautiful and useful. Crafts include print making, weaving, fabric design, ceramics and jewelry making."

If your child enjoys crafts, he will probably want to take a class or two while he is in high school. Some craft skills like pottery take three to five years to learn, while others can be learned in less than a year. Many crafts can be learned with local artisans, in night classes, or in videos or books. Each craft requires specific materials.

In this section, I will give a brief description of the materials your child will need to do each particular craft. Most require special materials and equipment that is not sold in art supply catalogs. There are several ways you can find out where to purchase the craft supplies: craft books usually have a section that tells you where to purchase the supplies; the reference librarian, art supply companies, and craft stores often know of other suppliers; a local craft or art guild can help; and, of course, the Yellow Pages of the nearest large city phone book are a great source. Two books you may find helpful are: *Directory of Mail Order Catalogs* by R. Gottlieb (Grey House Publishers) and *The Crafts Supply Sourcebook* by Margaret A. Boyd (Betterway Publications).

Many crafts can be self-taught, and the supplies listed below will give your child a good start. I would, however, like to recommend that he get instruction through books, videos, or private tutor. The best craftsmen not only have the skills necessary to create their craft, they have a good working knowledge and understanding of the elements of art and the principles of design.

WEAVING—This craft requires a loom. A beginner can use a cardboard loom for the first weaving and then progress to a two-harness or inkle loom. After he has mastered these types of weaving, he can get a table four-harness or a floor model loom. There are two types of string in a weaving—the warp and the weft. The warp threads are put on the loom, and the weft threads are woven in between them. The weft is usually the only threads you see in a weaving. The weft threads are passed through the warp threads by means of a shuttle, then gently pushed against the last row of yarn by a large-toothed comb. The basic skills of weaving on a loom can be learned through reading a book or with a teacher in approximately six months. To become a top quality weaver, you should study weaving for at least two years.

Item	Size, Weight, Quantity
Warp thread, beige and black	4-ply, 1 each color
Two- and four-harness table loom	18" x 70"
Flat shuttles	18", 3
Stainless steel scissors	7" and 5" or less, 1 of each size
Weaving yarn assortment	12 lbs.
Chipboard weaving loom	13" x 13"
OR Inkle loom	$12^1/_2$" weaving width

EMBROIDERY—Embroidery is simply decorating fabric by stitching thread into it. There are many different stitches, which can be learned through reading books or by lessons. The embroidery can be placed on any kind of material that will easily receive a needle. The fabric should be placed between two hoops that hold it tight so it can be easily stitched. The threads are usually thin so they will lie flat and not interfere with the original purpose of the material. If a project is to be framed, you can do it yourself or take it to a professional framer. Stretching cloth and getting it exactly square is very difficult and best left to someone with the proper equipment. Many a beautiful embroidery has been ruined by improper framing.

Item	Size, Weight, Quantity
Hardanger or 18 count Aida embroidery cloth, off white	48" wide
Embroidery needle assortment	Sizes 3-9

Fabric pen with disappearing ink	
Wood embroidery hoops	6", 10", 1 each size
Embroidery floss or pearl cotton	Size 5, set of 24 assorted colors

SOFT SCULPTURE, APPLIQUE, and QUILTING—These three crafts all require a good working knowledge of hand and machine sewing. Your local fabric stores carry most of the supplies. Quilting is best done with quilting needles, size 5 pearl cotton thread or quilting thread, a round or square frame to stretch the material being quilted, and regular sewing needles with a variety of eye sizes. The choice of material can be left up to the artist. A good clue to choosing compatible materials is to find those that each have one color in common.

Working with fabric requires special tools. He will need a pair of pinking shears and fabric scissors that will be used exclusively on cloth. He will also need an iron. All seams and hems should be ironed. Some other items that he might use are polyester fiberfill, washable felt, sequins, sew-on eyes, braid, lace, glue-on gemstones, buttons, beads, leather, embroidery floss, and metallic fabrics. With these materials your teen can make pillows, dolls, and banners. If he likes to work with fabric, keep a wide variety of materials to challenge his creativity. Although this craft is predominantly done by women, men enjoy it too and often are better at it.

Item	Size, Weight, Quantity
Assorted fabrics	5 yds.
Assorted needles	1 pkg.
Quilting needles	1 pkg.
Quilting thread	1 spool
Wooden hoops	12", 16", 1 each
Pinking shears	
Stainless steel scissors	7"
Polyester pillow form	10" x 10"
Thread to match fabric	3 spools
Iron	
Polyester fiberfill	1 bag
Embroidery floss	3 skeins
Sewing machine	

FABRIC DECORATION—If your child likes to dress well and enjoys art, he may enjoy fabric design. One of the oldest forms is called *batik*. Wax is applied to the fabric in designs and then the fabric is dyed another color. When the wax is removed, the original color is intact. He can also use textile paints in the form of markers, liquids, pastels, and crayons. The paints can be put on the fabric with stencils, airbrush, paintbrush, squeeze tubes, or by heating transfer paper. Many of the paints are set permanently into the fabric with heat. Some work better on natural fibers like cotton; others work best on synthetics. He can decorate jackets, T-shirts, jeans, canvas bags, work aprons, etc. For supplies, he will need paint and stencil brushes, scissors, transfer paper, sponges, stencils and a stencil-cutting pen, batik wax, and dyes.

Item	Size, Weight, Quantity
Pillow cases, 100% cotton	4
T-shirts, white	Large, 2
Batik liquid wax in a bottle	8 oz.
Cold water dyes	3
Cold water dye fix	3
Fabric markers	Set of 9
Stencil sheet	9" x 12", set of 10
Stencil stick spray adhesive	$4^3/_4$ oz.
Stencil brushes	$3/_4$", $1/_4$", 1 each size
Stencil cutting pen	

CERAMICS—Working with clay to make pottery and other functional items is called ceramics. For the most part, it requires baking the finished product in a kiln, and using a potter's wheel. Both the kiln and the wheel are very expensive and require a lot of skill to operate. If your teen wants to study ceramics, he is better off learning it privately or in a high school program from a professional potter. Hand-built pottery can be made at home but is extremely difficult to transport to a place where there is a kiln. Ceramics is a very difficult craft that requires three to five years to master. If he wants to work at home, provide the self-hardening or non-hardening varieties of clay.

Read the labels on all sculpture material to determine the health hazards. Manufacturers are becoming more health-conscious and warning their customers of special hazards.

MOBILES—Mobiles are moving sculptures that are usually suspended from the ceiling and move with the air currents in the room. If your child is fascinated by mobiles, you might consider getting the tools to work on one at home. The objects on the mobile must be lightweight and can be made from almost anything. They are suspended by wire and lightweight thread or fishing line. He may need a book or video on how to make them for a first try but will be able to do it himself after some practice.

Item	Size, Weight, Quantity
Galvanized wire	16 and 18 gauge, 50' coils
Long-nosed pliers	3-4
All-purpose utility snips	7"
Nylon fishing line	Lightweight, heavyweight, 1 each
Sheets of tin, such as "Tagger's tin".	006 and .012, 1 each size
Watercolor paper	22" x 30", 130 lb., 1 sheet
Balsa wood	6" x 12" x $^1/_{16}$", 1 sheet
Razor cutter	
Self-adhesive clear Contact® paper	
Scissors	

BASKETRY—Learning to make baskets is difficult on your own. You can rent videos and read books, but it is best to learn by taking a class or watching a professional basket maker. This craft can be learned in a month, but to be proficient in all forms of basketry will take a year or two. The supplies can be found in and around your home or can be purchased from crafts stores. Baskets are basically made from reed (a tall grass). The tools your child will need are natural or artificial reeds, a fid (used for separating strands of reed), and a pair of all-purpose utility snips. The reed is soaked until it bends easily and then woven into baskets. Supplies can be purchased at craft stores and through catalogs that offer craft supplies.

Item	Size, Weight, Quantity
Round dish basket kit	5"
Flat dish mat	7$^1/_2$" diameter
Fid	
All-purpose utility snips	

LEATHER—Working with leather requires special tools. Purchase a basic set of leather tools, some scraps of heavy leather, and a thick precut leather item like a comb holder, belt, or wallet that he can cut designs into after he has practiced on the scraps. He can learn leather craft on his own, but after he has practiced for a while, he will probably want some lessons. A good video or book will also be helpful to understanding the history of this craft and how to get professional results.

Item	Size, Weight, Quantity
Leather belt strip	$1^1/2$" x 45"
Awl	
Bawl tracer	
Revolving punch	
Leather craft tool set	
Snaps, black	Pkg. of 12
Carving leather pieces	2 lb. bag
Leather remnants	5 lb. box
Rawhide lacing leather	$1/8$" x 72"
Lacing needle	
Rawhide mallet	Size 1

JEWELRY—Jewelry made of metal requires tools that melt it and should therefore be done *only* with proper instruction. Learning the basic processes involved in making metal jewelry can be done in several months, but to get a good working knowledge of all the processes and materials can take as long as two years. Good instruction is highly recommended because of the many hazards involved in heating and casting metals.

Before investing in a class or private instruction, you might consider purchasing several varieties of plastic to make jewelry. They do not have to be heated to high temperatures and are an inexpensive way to test your child's interest in making jewelry.

Other crafts that use similar skills to create metal jewelry are: glass or aluminum etching, low-temperature enameling, and carving with wax. Below are some materials that can be made into jewelry but do not require expensive and dangerous equipment. A wide variety of materials will challenge creativity.

Item	Size, Weight, Quantity
Colored modeling material, oven-hardening	1 oz. each, set of 8
Plastic for jewelry making, softens in hot water	Small pkg.
Findings for earrings, bar pin, 24" necklace in cable and curb design (nickel-plated)	

Shrink art plastic sheets, clear	$8^1/4"$ x $10^3/4"$
Natural feathers, chicken and pheasant	
Indian bead assortment	$^5/_{16}$ oz.
Bead wire	24 yd. spool
Bead thread	225 yd. spool
Extra long Indian bead needles	Pkg. of 6
Aluminum etching powder	1 pint
Aluminum circle	8"
Aluminum rectangle	6" x 9"
Etching tools	Set of 3
Carving wax, brown	$3^1/2"$ block
Stainless steel wax modeling tools	Set of 5
Alcohol lamp for heating wax modeling tools	
Denatured alcohol for lamp	1 quart
Low temperature enameling oven and kit	
Macramé work board	
T-pins	$1^1/2"$ long, 100
Cotton cable twist cord	$^1/8"$, 1 lb. ball

Some Final Comments About Crafts

Your child's interest in crafts is best served when it is not limited by someone else's ideas as found in many books and pamphlets. It may be important to study their ideas and try a few just to understand the processes involved, but you should try to encourage your child's own ideas.

My personal journey with the craft of embroidery started with other people's ideas and instruction. I purchased a kit that gave me the entire design already on the material, showed me where to put each stitch, how to do the stitches, and exactly how it would look when it was done. When it was finished, I was so fascinated by this new art form that I found myself doing several other kits. However, I noticed a frustration building inside me as I labored through someone else's instructions. I was always thinking of better ways to do it. After three or four kits, I knew I loved embroidery and wanted to learn all I could about its history, techniques, and the artists creating embroidery in the '70s and '80s. The reference librarian and I found many books on the subject. One of the books described making house portraits with needlepoint and I decided that the same idea could be done in crewel embroidery. After several months, I finished an embroidery of my home. When my friend Bette saw it, she asked me to do hers. There was so much more satisfaction in creating my own embroidery that I continued making house portraits and started a small business.

Looking back, I am thankful to the producers of the kits. They gave me the supplies and instruction and courage to try embroidery. If your child would like to learn a craft by doing a kit first, this may be a good idea. If he really likes it, then you can purchase all the supplies he will need to work on his own.

You can best encourage your child, if he is interested in any craft, by providing good instruction, all the necessary supplies, interesting books or videos of other craftsmen, and by commending his neatness and praising his efforts when he uses creativity and knowledge of art to make the work his idea and not just a copy of someone else's work.

Basic Art Supplies for the 15 to 18 Year Old

Your child's interest in art, whether it is in the fine arts or crafts, will be strengthened if you offer some basic supplies. If he has a variety of tools and materials readily available, his chances of being creative are much better than if he has only the supplies for a particular medium. Many of the materials used in one art form can be used in another. New art forms are often a result of experiments involving a combination of materials never before thought compatible.

Below is a list of the basic art supplies that a fifteen to eighteen year old would enjoy having in his studio. Keep in mind that these are just a few of the many art supplies available. As your child studies a specific medium in depth, he will use some of these materials and purchase others.

Item	Size, Weight, Quantity
Acrylic paints	2 oz. jars, set of 12
Gesso	1 pint
Matte varnish	1 pint
Paint brushes, round	Sizes 00, 1, 10
Paint brushes, brights	Sizes 2, 8
Paint brush, flat	Size 4
Paint brushes, budget one-use style	#2, 12
Foam brushes	2", 10
Brush tub with brush holders	

Metal or wood table easel	
Denim apron	30"
Sulphite drawing paper	80 lb., 1 pad
Colored sculpture paper	$9^1/2$" x $12^1/2$", 24 sheet pad
Art tissue paper	Asstd. 20" x 30", 20 sheets
Metallic paper, 5 colors	10" x 13"
Origami paper	$4^5/8$" square, 40 sheets
Origami paper	6" square, 16 sheet
Rough drawing paper sketch pads	50 lb., 8" x 11", 2
Pocket sketchbook	$3^1/2$" x $4^3/4$", 80 sheets
Blank greeting cards/envelopes	$4^3/8$" x $5^3/4$", 10
Railroad poster board, buff	6-ply, 22" x 28", 10 sheets
Retractable blade knife with four positions	
Blades for utility knife	Pkg. of 5
Stainless steel scissors	$4^1/2$" and 7", 1 pair of each
White super thick glue	4 oz.
Sobo glue	4 oz.
Wood glue	4 oz.
Glue for non-porous materials	$5/8$ oz. tube
Masking tape	$3/4$"
Removable transparent tape	$1/2$"
Paper punch	$1/4$"
Stapler	$3^3/4$" throat
Staples	
Pocket lead pointer with container	
Kneaded eraser	
Vinyl eraser	
Soap eraser	
Drawing pencils	Sizes 2B, 4B, 6B
Colored pencils	Set of 40-60
Peel-off charcoal pencil, soft	
Plastic crayons	Set of 24
Watercolor markers, fine point	Set of 8
Broad-tip fluorescent markers	Set of 4
Watercolor black marker, extra-fine and regular	1 each
Permanent black marker, fine-tip	
Calligraphy pen	Set of 3
Draftsman's brush	2"
Plastic triangle	10"
Stainless steel inking ruler	18"
T-square	
Yardstick	
Protractor	

Bow compass, heavy-duty	$4^1/2$"
Grid paper with non-reproducible ink	10" x 20", 50 sheet pad
Sponge—elephant ear, small	
Plastic sculpture	5" asstd., $^1/_2$ lb. color sticks
Long-nose pliers	$6^1/2$" and diagonal cut, 1 each
All-purpose utility snips	7"
Ball peen hammer	8 oz.
Sandpaper assortment	9" x 10", 15 sheets
Steel wool	Very fine #00
Sewing needle assortment, tapestry to darners	
Monk's cloth	4 x 4 weave, 1 yd.
Remnant yarn assortment	5 lb.
Embroidery floss	6 strand, 24 asstd. colors
Cotton cable twist cord	$^1/_{16}$", $^1/_8$", 1 lb. ball of each
Polyester fiberfill	1 lb. bag
Basswood scrap bag	
Keyhole saw	10-12"
Curved blade tweezers	7"
Galvanized steel wire	24 gauge
Asstd. medium wood beads	1 lb.
Macramé work board with squares	12" x 19" x $^1/_2$"
Warp thread	1 spool

10.

JUST FOR GRANDPARENTS

As a grandparent, you have a very special role in the life of your grandchild. Unfortunately, there has not been enough written about the role of a grandparent, perhaps because it is so easy to be one. Our many years of making countless mistakes with our own children make us more understanding and less critical. To your grandchild, you are a very special person. When I taught school, grandmas and grandpas were spoken of in the highest of terms. I was told, "She's my very best friend," and "Papaw took me to a place where they had lots of rides, we even got to go on the bumper cars. I love him so much!" and "This picture is for my grandma. You know what, Mrs. Wilder (my former name)? She takes some of my pictures to work so everyone can see them." Bubbles, sparkle, and a big brass band would seem to burst from their eyes as they spoke about their grandparents. A calm filled their energetic little bodies as they remembered what it's like to be with their grandparents.

Even the older students expressed a deep love and affection for their grandparents. For them, the anxiety brought on by the pressure of school, their need to begin the process of breaking away from their parents, and peer pressure would quickly disappear as they thought about their grandparents. Children know you love them unconditionally and are always proud of their achievements no matter how insignificant they are to the rest of the world. You play a very special role that no one else can fill in a child's life. You are a treasure to your grandchild.

This special relationship between you and your grandchild can be used to help her develop her artistic talent. Her parents are so busy trying to handle the daily necessities of running the family that they may sometimes fail to see a budding talent in their child. Perhaps you were the first one to notice your grandchild's talent in art. The question now is, what can you do without interfering with the parents' methods of child rearing? Here are a few suggestions.

- Give your grandchild art-related presents, such as a pad of paper, crayons, paints, an easel, or even an art book—instead of toys.
- Offer to take her to an art class after school or on Saturdays.
- When she visits, let her do art activities that her parents may not permit, such as painting, cutting paper, or using clay.
- Take her to the library to look at art books. Make sure she reads (or has read to her) all the books that have won a Caldecott medal (an award given for outstanding illustrations in children's books). You might even make this your weekly or monthly outing with your grandchild.
- Get her a subscription to a magazine that is full of good artwork, beautiful photographs, and/or has art-related activities.
- If your grandchild likes to draw a specific subject, such as horses, give her a sculpture or picture of the subject.
- Take her to a local art fair or an art museum.
- Hang her pictures in your home or take one to work.
- Have one of her pictures professionally framed and hang it next to the other artwork in your home.
- Send her postcards with famous artwork on them.
- Purchase art materials and furnishings that perhaps her parents cannot afford.
- Offer to babysit her siblings, so her parents can take her to an art-related activity.
- Provide an area in your home where she can work on art.
- Send her a big box of drawing paper.
- If you live far away, send her some large, self-addressed envelopes so she can send you her artwork.
- If your grandchild enjoys entering art contests, watch for

them and send her the details on entering.

- Sign up for an art class yourself. A good friend of mine took her first art lesson at age sixty-eight. She is now eighty-five, has shown remarkable talent, and thoroughly enjoys the challenges of art. You and your grandchild can help each other learn about art.
- Books are an important resource for a child learning art. When she owns her own books, she can study them as questions arise. She will need how-to books on her specific area of interest, art history books, and a book that explains the elements of art and the principles of design.

Your role as grandparent can be very rewarding and fulfilling when you fill any gaps left by parents who are sometimes too busy to help their children. Schools and people outside the family can help, but those people whom a child really loves are the most influential. Even the most talented child can lose interest in art when she is not encouraged by her family. You can recognize just how precious a talent can be, especially when it results in success. If you see a talent in your grandchild, speak to her parents about it and tell them you would like to help and how you want to do it.

When there are many grandchildren and you do not want to play favorites, the decision to help just one becomes more difficult. But you must also keep in mind that doing nothing may result in another talented child lost in the shuffle of life. If you only have energy and patience enough for one grandchild, it may be better to take that one and concentrate your energies on her. If one grandchild is talented in art and you want to help her, trust the love that your other grandchildren have for you. It will help them know in their hearts that your guidance of their brother will produce someone they will someday be very proud of. They, too, may someday get that extra attention; and perhaps they will learn that one of life's greatest joys is not in receiving but in giving.

Grandchildren realize instinctively that you know more about life than their parents. They may come to you for advice before they will their parents. Sam Levenson said, "The reason grandparents and grandchildren get along so well is that they have a common enemy." I'm not sure I agree with him, but it does have a familiar ring. Learning art is much like learning other skills; it takes a lot of hard work and self-confidence. Although you, yourself, may not be an artist, many of the experiences in your life will help your grandchild understand the difficulties in learning art.

One of the most important things you can do for your grandchild is to give her reassurance. Tell her that art is very difficult, even for the most talented child. If she says she can't do it, remind her that it is better to say it is hard to do. Remind her of all the hard things she has learned in the past and tell her about the times you struggled and even mention the times you failed. She needs to know that in order to learn anything, she must think she can do it. Art is not easy, it presents many challenges: perfection is almost impossible; there is so much to learn that she will never learn it all; and she will never be totally satisfied with her work. The good news is she can learn parts of it and be really good at them. She can learn how to paint with watercolors, how to carve wood, and how to weave a blanket. There is always something new to learn when you are an artist. You might also mention how you admire her interest in art and how happy you are that she has such strong feelings about art; it will make her entire life so much more interesting.

Treasure your grandchild's talent in art. Use your time, money, and knowledge to help her develop art skills. Let her use that interest and drive she has for art to show her just what good hard work can produce. Perhaps you even agree with Emily Dickinson: "Luck is not chance, It's Toil, Fortune's expensive smile is earned." Whether you can give a few hours a week, a half hour a month, or have to communicate through the mail, make a *commitment* to your artistic grandchild that you will help her in any way possible to develop her artistic talent. She won't love you any more for it, because she already loves you unconditionally, but perhaps you will find great satisfaction someday knowing that without your support, she might never have developed her talent in art.

APPENDICES

1. ART SUPPLY STORES AND CATALOGS

One of the most frequently asked questions is, "Where can I get good art supplies?" The first place to look is your local art supply store. If you cannot find what you want there, you can request your art materials from one of the companies listed in this chapter. Most offer catalogs, but there is usually a small charge to cover printing and mailing costs. Most companies will supply their catalog free with $50 or more orders. All the companies listed below have expressed their eagerness to help you and your child obtain art supplies.

ABEL FRAME AND ART SUPPLY INC.
4848 Virginia Beach Blvd.
Virginia Beach, VA 23462
(804) 497-6949

No catalog. Offers customers fine art, graphic, sculpture, drafting, and architectural supplies. Also offers framing materials and good selection of art books.

AMERICAN ART CLAY
4717 W. 16th St.
Indianapolis, IN 46222
(317) 244-6871

Catalog company and retail store that sells kilns, wheels, and equipment; clays, glazes, underglazes, brushes, tools, and supplies; glass and metal enameling supplies, sculpture materials, etc. Beautiful catalog with moderately priced sculpture materials.

ART MATERIALS INCORPORATED
3018 Lyndale Ave. S
Minneapolis, MN 55408
(612) 827-5301
ALSO: 315 14th Ave. SE
Minneapolis, MN 55414
(612) 331-6864

Catalog features paper, framing supplies, drawing and sketching supplies, paints, painting accessories, brushes, airbrush equipment, cutting tools, drafting supplies, templates, sculpture modeling supplies, art furniture, etc. Professional and amateur quality materials with moderate prices.

THE ART STORE
7301 Beverly Blvd.
Los Angeles, CA 90036
(213) 933-9286

Other store locations in California are Hollywood, West L.A., Pasadena, Universal City, Irvine, Fullerton, San Francisco, and the Student Store in Los Angeles. Colorado has two stores — one in Berkeley and one in Denver.

Catalog and retail sales of brushes, paints, canvas, papers, pens, drawing and drafting supplies, studio furniture, templates, graphic arts accessories, print making supplies, clays, framing supplies, books, etc. Good quality art supplies with moderate to low prices.

BATES
4901 Century Plaza Rd.
Indianapolis, IN 46254
(317) 297-8000

Retail store and catalog feature pens, pencils, markers, adhesives, paper, drawing supplies, fine art materials, portfolios, architectural modeling supplies, templates, tools, books, pressure graphics, computer plotter supplies, office supplies, projection and visual display materials, etc.

BOUTILIER'S ART CENTER
900 Church St.
Burlington, VT 05401
(802) 864-5475

No catalog. Store carries painting, sculpture, drawing, calligraphy, silkscreen, drafting, graphic arts materials, and quality children's art supplies. Competitive prices and knowledgeable and friendly staff.

COLOR CRAFT
4759 East Speedway
Tucson, AZ 85712
(602) 327-6553

Catalog features art supplies for the advanced artist and professional. They offer a wide range of top quality art materials.

DENVER ART SUPPLY
1437 California St.
Denver, CO 80202-4212
(303) 534-1437

Catalog features brushes, paints, canvas supplies, papers, pens, drawing and drafting supplies, studio furniture, templates, print making supplies, art and craft supplies for young children, clays and modeling materials, books, etc. Excellent catalog for professional and amateur. Each customer is assured individual service. The store offers art materials that "foster excitement and encourage the creative process," say David Pyle, store manager. They also carry new and unusual supplies in their store that are not listed in the catalog. This company is interested in not only selling to the public but educating them through seminars in their store and technical information throughout the catalog.

DICK BLICK WEST
P.O. Box 521
Henderson, NV 89015
(702) 451-7662

DICK BLICK CENTRAL
P.O. Box 1267
Galesburg, IL 61401
(309) 343-6181

DICK BLICK EAST
P.O. Box 26
Allentown, PA 18105
(215) 965-6051

Supplies art materials for beginning artist and craftsperson as well as professionals. Catalog features paints; brushes; papers; framing supplies; drawing supplies; airbrushes; graphic art materials; screen printing, print making, woodworking, and sculpture supplies; cutting tools; sign supplies; furniture; easels; shop tools; books, etc.

DMI INDUSTRIES INC.
1201 E. Whitcomb
Madison Heights, MI 48071
(313) 385-1490

Other retail locations in Ann Arbor, Dearborn, and Royal Oak, Michigan. Catalog features items for the art and engineering student and professional. DMI offers a wide range of fine art materials, art furniture, drafting supplies, picture framing, etc.

DUNBART ART SUPPLIES
4129 Magnolia St.
New Orleans, LA 70115
(504) 895-7594

Selling area is all of Louisiana and southern Mississippi. Dunbart gives its customers flyers instead of a catalog. They offer a wide range of art supplies from paints to frames at discount prices.

A.I. FRIEDMAN
44 W. 18th St.
New York, NY 10011
(212) 243-9000

Other stores in New York City and Port Chester, New York. Stores and catalogs feature art furniture, papers, art cases, adhesives, office supplies, markers, pencils, pens, paints, graphic design supplies, cutting tools, brushes, airbrush supplies, framing supplies, books, etc. Professional quality art supplies at moderate prices.

INDIANA CLAY COMPANY
104 Main St
P.O. Box 332
Battleground, IN 47920
(317) 567-2774

Sales mainly through catalog. Small business owned by two dedicated and hard-working men who are eager to share their knowledge and assist customers with their products. They sell clay, chemicals, equipment, and tools.

J.S. LATTA COMPANY
2218 Main St.
Box 128
Cedar Falls, IA 50613
(319) 266-3501

Catalog company that services public and schools. Art materials mainly geared to the young student. Offers a good selection of yarns for beginning weavers.

MACCO OF BETHESDA
8311 Wisconsin Ave. A-1
Bethesda, MD 20814
(301) 656-7749

Family-run business since 1949; no catalog. Located near Washington, DC. They pride themselves on knowledgeable service to customers as well as an extensive line of quality art products from student to professional quality. Carries some obscure items no longer available elsewhere.

MICHAELS
5931 Campus Circle Dr.
Las Colinas Business Park
Irving, TX 75063

Chain store with no catalog. Stores in Alabama, Arizona, Arkansas, California, Colorado, Georgia, Illinois, Indiana, Kansas, Louisiana, Missouri, Nevada, New Mexico, North Carolina, South Carolina, Tennessee, and Texas.

This store offers supplies mainly for people interested in crafts. They offer creative crafts; frames; silk and dried flowers; art, hobby, stitchery, and wedding supplies, as well as seasonal goods, miniatures, hobby supplies, etc. Some stores offer classes and have a Saturday kids' corner.

NASCO ARTS AND CRAFTS
901 Janesville Ave.
Fort Atkinson, WI 53538-0901
(414) 563-2446

NASCO WEST
1524 Princeton Ave.
Modesto, CA 95352-3837
(209) 529-6957

Catalog and retail stores offering a wide array of art materials. This company is used a lot by art teachers because they offer moderately priced fine art and craft materials for beginning artists. Nasco offers painting supplies; sculpture materials; art furniture; paper; woodcraft, modeling, decorative, tole, rosemaling, jewelry, metal enameling, metal tooling, etching, leather, beads, basketry, and weaving supplies; fabrics and dyes; decorator craft; stained glass, etc. They carry basic materials for the beginning artist and craftsman.

NORTHWEST DRAWING AND VANART
1290 Northwest Hwy.
Des Plaines, IL 60016
(708) 824-5800
ANOTHER RETAIL STORE AT:
418 S. Wabash
Chicago, IL 60506
(312) 922-5816

Art supplies for the professional artist. They carry graphic art materials, paper, painting media, brushes, easels, pencils, pens, cutting tools, airbrush supplies, tapes, drafting equipment and supplies, sculpture materials, books, plotter and computer supplies, etc.

SAX ARTS AND CRAFTS
P.O. Box 15710
New Berlin, WI 53151
(414) 784-6880
EASTERN BRANCH:
P.O. Box 2511
Allentown, PA 18001
(215) 395-8531
SOUTHWESTERN BRANCH:
P.O. Box 95039
Arlington, TX 76005
(817) 640-0009

Offers a wide range of materials for the beginning artist at moderate prices. Sax offers paints, brushes, paper, crayons, markers, pens, furniture, print making supplies, books, ceramic supplies, sculpture materials, art metals, leather crafts supplies, looms, yarn and fiber art supplies, basketry supplies, fabric decorating materials, candlemaking supplies, etc.

STANDARD BLUE AND ARTWORLD
924 Grand Ave.
Des Moines, IA 50309
(515) 288-1927

Other store locations in Nebraska and Kansas. Offers fine art and professional art supplies: paints; brushes; airbrush, young artists', print making, sculpture, ceramic supplies; markers, pencils, drafting supplies; paper; framing and office supplies; cutting tools; graphic art supplies; furniture; books, etc.

DANIEL SMITH
4130 First Ave. S
Seattle, WA 98134-2302
(206) 223-9599

Catalog company with one retail store in Washington offering high quality paper including exotic and Japanese papers. Watercolor, gouache, oil, alkyd, acrylic, and tempera paints. Also brushes, canvas, framing, airbrush supplies, dry pigments and metallic ieafing, pastels, drawing and graphic supplies, furniture, print making supplies, and books. This is a company that features top-of-the-line materials for the serious artist. Friendly, individualized customer service with an unconditional guarantee on all products. Beautiful and educational catalog.

TRIARCO ARTS AND CRAFTS INC.
14650 28th Ave. N
Plymouth, MN 55447
(612) 559-5590

Catalog is used by art educators because of the competitive pricing and wide selection of books and supplies for fine art, sculpture, painting, ceramics, weaving, batik, textile crafts, airbrush, jewelry making, silkscreen, block printing, woodcraft, tile work, etc. Good selection of materials for beginning arts and crafts people.

ZIM'S INC.
4370 South 300 West
Salt Lake City, UT 84107
(801) 268-2505

Large retail craft store that will sell through the mail. If you cannot find what you want in your local craft store, write or call Zim's. Catalog is very large and is expensive to provide to all customers. They will, however, be happy to send you a listing of specific craft items. Zim's carries a large selection of wood craft patterns to paint or stain, wood boxes, porcelain figures and boxes, papier maché figures, painting supplies, stencils, paper, mat boards, craft instruction books, doll supplies, cross stitch and needlepoint fabric, embroidery thread and some yarn, thread, lace trim and ribbon, macramé cord and accessories, doll house accessories, miniatures, flower-making supplies, candy and cake supplies, wedding supplies, music boxes, clock parts, etc. This is not a wholesaler; prices are comparable to local retail shops.

The companies listed in this section do not represent all the companies and stores in the U.S. that carry art supplies. Check your local telephone directory for stores in your area.

2. RECOMMENDED READING FOR YOUNG ARTISTS

In this section I recommend some of the best art books available in libraries and book stores for children ages five to fourteen. There are many other good art books for your child; this is only a partial list. I am only recommending books *I* have read. Try to keep a wide variety of art books available to your child at all times.

All the books listed below were found in libraries in my area. If your library does not have the book you want, have your librarian get it for you through an inter-library loan. You can also order it from your local book store if it is still in print. Your child will appreciate assistance from you and the librarian in finding the books he needs. Your child needs not only art supplies to pursue his artistic goals, he needs good art books.

NOTE: Books for young readers (5-7) are marked with a ✓.

Architecture

Adkins, Jan. *How a House Happens*. Walker and Co., 1972.

Giblin, James Cross. *The Skyscraper Book*. Crowell, 1981.

Downer, Marion. *Roofs Over America*. Lothrop, Lee and Shepard Co., 1967.

Hiller, Carl. *Caves to Cathedrals*. Little, Brown and Co., 1974.

Hoag, Edwin. *American Houses*. J.B. Lippincott Company, 1964.

Huey, E.G. and V.M. Hillyer. *Architecture, A Young People's Story of Our Heritage: 3,000 B.C. to Gothic*. Meredith Press, 1966.

_____. *Architecture, A Young People's Story of Our Heritage: Gothic to Modern*. Meredith Press, 1966.

Isaacson, Philip M. *Round Buildings, Square Buildings, and Buildings that Wiggle Like a Fish*. Alfred E. Knopf, 1988.

Lamprey, L. *All the Ways of Building*., Macmillan, 1933.

Leacraft, Richard and Helen Leacraft. *Buildings of Ancient Egypt*. Wm. R. Scott Inc., 1963.

Macaulay, David. *Castle*. Houghton Mifflin, 1973.

_____. *Cathedral*. Houghton Mifflin, 1973.

Pennock, Lee. *Americans at Home*. Huntington, 1981.

✓Sharr, Christine. *Homes*. Grosset and Dunlap, 1972.

Art History and Appreciation

Borten, Helen. *A Picture Has A Special Look*. Abelard-Schuman, 1961.

Cunning, Robert. *Just Look. A Book About Paintings*. Charles Scribner's Sons, 1979.

Hillyer, V.M. and E.G. Huey. *Fine Art, Young People's Story of Our Heritage*. Meredith Press, 1966. (Series of books covering 1500 B.C. to 1800 A.D.: *Etruscans, Ancient Rome, Egypt, Africa, Lands of the Bible, Japan, India, Eskimos, Colonial America, Spanish in America and Puerto Rico*, and *The Last 200 Years*.)

Holmes, Bryan. *Creatures of Paradise*. Oxford University Press, 1980.

Marshall, Anthony D. *Africa's Living Arts*. Franklin Watts Inc., 1970.

Witty, Ken. *Day in the Life of an Illustrator*. Troll Assoc., 1970.

Crafts

Anderson, Mildred. *Papier Maché Crafts*. Sterling Publ. Co. Inc., 1975.

Cartner, William C. *The Young Calligrapher*. Frederick Warne and Co., 1969.

Choate, Judith and Jane Green. *Patchwork*. Doubleday and Co., 1976.

Cone, Ferne Geller. *Knutty Knitting for Kids*. Follett Publ. Co., 1977.

Dodd, Xenia Ley Parker. *A Beginner's Book of Off-Loom Weaving*. Mead and Co., 1975.

Felicity, Everett. *Usborne's Make Your Own Jewelry*. EDC Publ., 1987.

Grol, Lini. *Scissorcraft*. Sterling Publ., 1970.

Hodgson, Mary Anne and Josephine Ruth Paine. *Fast and Easy Needlepoint*. Doubleday and Co., 1978.

Hofsinde, Robert. *Indian Beadwork*. William Morrow and Co., 1958.

Holz, Loretta. *Mobiles You Can Make*. Lothrop, Lee and Shepard Co., 1975.

Ickis, Marguerite. *Weaving as a Hobby*. Sterling Publ. Co., 1968.

Johnson, Sally. *Traditional Lacemaking*. Van Nostrand Reinhold Co., 1964.

Kelly, Karin. *Weaving*. Lerner Publ. Co., 1973.

Lancaster, John. *Lettering*. Franklin Watts, 1988.

Lasky, Kathryn. *The Weaver's Gift*. Frederick Warne and Co., 1980.

Lee, Ruth and Mary Gehr. *Exploring the World of Pottery*. Children's Press, 1967.

Leeming, Joseph. *Fun With Leather*. J.B. Lippincott Co., 1941.

Meyer, Carolyn. *Stitch By Stitch, Needlework for Beginners*. Harcourt Brace Jovanovich Inc., 1970.

Nicklaus, Carol. *Making Dolls*. Franklin Watts, 1981.

Parish, Peggy. *Beginning Mobiles*. Macmillan Publ. Co., 1979.

Phillips, Mary Walker. *Knitting*. Franklin Watts, 1977.

_____. *Step-by-Step Macramé*. Golden Press, 1970.

Potter, Tony. *Usborne's Guide to Pottery from Start to Finish*. EDC Publ. 1986.

Rubenstone, Jessie. *Knitting for Beginners*. J.B. Lippincott, 1973.

Schal, Hannelore and Ulla Abdalla. *Toys Made Of Clay*. Children's Press, 1990.

Sommer, Else. *A Patchwork, Appliqué and Quilting Primer*. Lothrop, Lee and Shepard Co., 1975.

VonWartburg, Ursula. *The Workshop Book of Knitting*. Atheneum, 1973.

Young, Eleanor R. *Crewel Embroidery*. Franklin Watts, 1976.

Zubrowski, Bernie. *Tops: Building and Experimenting with Spinning Toys*. Boston Children's Museum Activity Book, 1989.

Drawing and Painting

Adams, Norman and Joe Singer. *Drawing Animals*. Watson-Guptill, 1979.

Ames, Lee J. *Draw Fifty Animals*. Doubleday and Co. Inc., 1974.

Mr. Ames has also published drawing books on dogs, dinosaurs, cats, famous faces, holiday decorations, horses, star wars heroes, creatures, and spaceships.

Arnosky, Jim. *Sketching Outdoors in Spring*. Lothrop, Lee and Shepard, 1987.

Mr. Arnosky has also published drawing books on sketching in summer, fall, and winter.

Baxter, Leon. *The Drawing Book*. Ideals Children's Books, 1988.

Benjamin, Lea. *Cartooning for Kids*. Crowell, 1982.

Bolognese, Don and Elaine Raphael. *Charcoal and Pastel*. Franklin Watts, 1986.

Davidow, Ann H. *Let's Draw Animals*. Grosset and Dunlap, 1890.

Davis, Carolyn and Charlene Brown. *Color Fun, How to Use Color*. Walter Foster Publ., 1988.

Devonshire, Hilary. *Drawing*. Franklin Watts, 1990.

Emberley, Ed. *Big Green Drawing Book*. Little, Brown and Co., 1979.

Mr. Emberley has also published drawing books for very young readers entitled: *Drawing Book of Animals, Drawing Book of Faces, Make a World Drawing Book, Big Orange Drawing Book of Halloween, Great Thumbprint Drawing Book*, and *Picture Pie: A Circle Drawing Book*.

Emberley, Michael. *Dinosaurs*. Little, Brown and Co., 1980.

✓Emberley, Rebecca. *Drawing With Letters and Numbers*. Little, Brown and Co., 1982.

Foster, Patricia. *Usborne's Painting Book*. EDC Publ., 1981.

Frame, Paul. *Drawing the Big Cats*. Franklin Watts, 1981.

Mr. Frame has also written Drawing books about dogs and puppies, reptiles, sharks, whales, dolphins, and seals.

Hawkinson, John. *More to Collect and Paint from Nature* (watercolor painting). Albert Whitman and Co., 1964.

Hoff, Syd. *The ABC's of Cartooning*. G.P. Putnam;s Sons, 1972.

_____. *Jokes to Enjoy, Draw and Tell*. G.P. Putnam's Sons, 1974.

Hogeboom, Amy. *Familiar Animals and How to Draw Them*. Vanguard, 1946.

_____. *Forest Animals and How to Draw Them*. Vanguard, 1950.

✓Katz, Marjorie. *Fingerprint Owls and Other Fantasies*. M. Evans and Co. Inc., 1972.

Kistler, Mark. *Draw Squad*. Simon and Schuster, Inc., 1988. (Excellent how-to-draw book taken from a television series.)

✓Palazzo, Tony. *The Magic Crayon, Drawing from Simple Shapes and Forms*. The Lion Press, 1967.

Pluckrose, Henry. Paints. Franklin Watts, 1987.

Rauch, Hans George. *The Lines Are Coming*. Charles Scribner's Sons, 1978.

Savitt, Sam. *Draw Horses With Sam Savitt*. Viking Press, 1981.

Smith, Frank. *How to Draw Dinosaurs*. Scholastic Inc., 1984.

_____. *How to Draw Cats and Kittens*. Scholastic Inc., 1985.

✓Spilka, Arnold. *Paint All Kinds of Pictures*. Henry Z. Walck, 1963.

Tatchell, Judy. *Usborne's How to Draw Cartoons and Caricatures*. EDC Publ., 1987.

Weiss, Harvey. *Cartoons and Cartooning*. Houghton-Mifflin Co., 1990.

Zaidenberg, Arthur. *How to Draw Heads and Faces*. Abelard-Schuman, 1966.

Sculpture

✓Chernoff, Goldie Taub. *Just a Box*. Walker and Co., 1973.

✓_____. *Clay Dough—Play Dough*. Walker and Co., 1973.

Felicity, Everett. *Usborne's Make Your Own Jewelry*. EDC Publ., 1987.

Hillyer, V.M. and E.G. Huey. *Sculpture, Young People's Story of Our Heritage*. Meredith Press, 1966.

Hull, Jeannie. *Clay*. Franklin Watts, 1989.

✓Kohl, MaryAnn. *Mud Works*. Bright Ring Publishing, 1989.

Lidstone, John. *Building With Balsa Wood*. D. Van Nostrand Co. Inc., 1965

_____. *Building With Cardboard*. D. Van Nostrand Co. Inc., 1968.

Maestro, Giulio and Betsy Maestro. *The Story of the Statue of Liberty*. Lothrop, Lee and Shepard, 1986.

Nakano, Dukuohtei. *Easy Origami*. Viking Kestrel, 1985.

Paine, Roberta M. *Looking at Sculpture*. Lothrop, Lee and Shepard Co. Inc., 1968.

✓Pitcher, Caroline. *Build Your Own Space Station*. Franklin Watts, 1985.

Reid, Barbara. *Playing With Plasticine*. Morrow Junior Books, 1988.

Reiger, Shay. *The Bronze Zoo*. Charles Scribner's Sons, 1970.

St. George, Judith. *Mount Rushmore Story*. G.P. Putnam's Sons, 1985.

Shapiro, Mary J. *How They Built the Statue of Liberty*. Random House, 1985.

Weiss, Harvey. *Carving—How to Carve Wood and Stone*. Addison-Wesley, 1976.

_____. *Collage and Construction*. Young Scott Books, 1970.

✓West, Robin. *Far Out, How to Create Your Own Starworld*. Carolrhoda Books, Inc., 1978.

Miscellaneous

✓Arnold, Wesley F. *Fun With Next to Nothing*. Harper and Row, 1962.

Arkins, Jan. *The Letterbox*. Walker Publ. Co., 1981.

Araki, Chiyo. *Origami in the Classroom*. Charles and Tuttle Co., 1965.

Arnold, Arnold. *The Crowell Book of Arts and Crafts for Children*. Thomas Y. Crowell Co., 1975.

Borja, Robert and Corinne Borja. *Making Chinese Papercuts*. Albert Whitman and Co., 1980.

✔Borten, Helen. *Do You See What I See*. E.M. Hale and Co., 1959.

Butterfield, Moira. *Usborne's Photography*. EDC Publ., 1987.

✔Caney, Steven. *Play Book*. Workman Pub. Co., 1975.

✔Cartlidge, Michelle. *The Bears' Bazaar, A Story Craft Book*. Lothrop, Lee and Shepard, 1979.

Chernoff, Goldie Taub. *Easy Costumes You Don't Have to Sew*. Four Winds Press, 1975.

Churchill, E. Richard. *Instant Paper Airplanes*. Sterling Publ. Co., 1988.

✔Conway, Judith. *Happy Haunting: Halloween Costumes You Can Make*. Troll Assoc., 1986.

Ms. Conway also wrote: *Things That Go and How to Make Toy Boats, Cars and Planes, Great Gifts to Make*.

Cramblit, Joella and JoAnn Loebel. *Flowers Are for Keeping: How to Dry Flowers and Make Gifts and Decorations*. Julian Messner, 1979.

✔Davis, Carolyn. *Poster Lettering Fun*. Walter Foster Publ. Co., 1988.

Eaton, Marge. *Flower Pressing*. Lerner Publ. Co., 1973.

✔Ehlert, Lois. *Color Zoo*. J.B. Lippincott, 1989.

Eisner, Vivienne and Adelle Weiss. *A Boat, A Bat, and A Beanie, Things to Make From Newspaper*. Lothrop, Lee and Shepard Co., 1977.

Feller, Ron and Marsha Feller. *Paper Masks and Puppets for Stories, Songs, and Plays*. The Arts Factory, 1985.

✔Fiarotta, Phyllis. *Snips and Snails and Walnut Whales: Nature Crafts for Children*. Workman Publ. Co., 1975.

Giles, Nancy. *Creative Food Box Crafts*. Good Apple Inc., 1989.

Haldane, Suzanne. *Painting Faces*. E.P. Dutton, 1988.

Hammett, Catherine. *Creative Crafts for Campers*. Association Press, 1957.

Hautzig, Esther. *Let's Make More Presents*. Macmillan Publ. Co. Inc., 1962.

Ickis, Marguerite. *Arts and Crafts, A Practical Handbook.* A.S. Barnes and Co., 1943.

Jordan, Nina. *American Costume Dolls, How to Make and Dress Them.* Harcourt Brace and Co., 1941. Also: *American Dolls in Uniform.*

Kinseer, Charleen. *Outdoor Art for Kids.* Follett Publ., 1975.

Klimo, Joan F. *What Can I Make Today: Sculpting, Printing, Pasting, Stitching, Decorating.* Pantheon Books, 1971.

Kohn, Bernice. *The Beachcomber's Book of Handicrafts.* Viking Press, 1970.

Leeming, Joseph. *Fun With Greeting Cards.* J.B. Lippincott Co., 1960.

✓Lopshire, Robert. *How to Make Flibbers, etc.: A Book of Things to Make and Do.* Random House, 1964.

✓_____. *How to Make Snop Snappers and Other Fine Things.* Greenwillow Books, 1977.

Lynch-Watson, Janet. *The Shadow Puppet Book.* Sterling Co. Inc., 1980.

✓MacAgy, Douglas and Elizabeth MacAgy. *Going For A Walk With A Line: A Step Into the World of Modern Art.* Doubleday and Co., 1959.

McClure, Nancee. *Free and Inexpensive Arts and Crafts to Make.* Good Apple Inc., 1987.

Meyer, Carolyn. *Yarn — The Things It Makes and How to Make Them.* Harcourt Brace Jovanovich Inc., 1972.

_____. *Rock Tumbling.* William Morrow and Co., 1975.

Munari, Bruno. *A Flower With Love: Flower Arranging.* Thomas Crowell Co., 1973.

Nicklaus, Carol. *Flying, Gliding and Whirling—Making Things That Fly.* Franklin Watts, 1981.

Parish, Peggy. *Costumes to Make.* Macmillan Publ. Co., 1977.

✓Perry, Margaret. *Rainy Day Magic: How to Make Sunshine On a Stormy Day.* Random House, 1964.

Pflug, Betsy. *You Can: Things to Make From Cans.* Van Nostrand Reinhold Co., 1969.

Polquin, Genevieve. *Cork Toys You Can Make.* Sterling Publ. Co. Inc., 1974.

Potter, Tony. *Usborne's Lettering and Typography.* EDC Publ. Co., 1987.

Purdy, Susan. *Holiday Cards for You to Make*. J.B. Lippincott Co., 1960.

✓Rockwell, Harlow. *I Did It*. Macmillan, 1974.

✓_____. *Look At This*. Macmillan, 1975.

Rourke, Arlene C. *Decorating Your Room*. Rourke Publ. Inc., 1989.

Seidelman, James E. and Grace Mintonye. *Creating Mosaics*. Macmillan, 1967.

Slade, Richard. *You Can Make a String Puppet*. John Watts, 1966.

Sommer, Else. *The Bread Dough Craft Book*. Lothrop, Lee and Shepard Co., 1972.

Storm, Betsy. *I Can Be An Interior Designer*. Children's Press, 1989.

✓Supraner, Robyn. *Fun to Make Nature Crafts*. Troll Assoc., 1981.

_____. *Fun With Paper*. Troll Assoc., 1981.

Taber, Gladys. *Flower Arranging: A Book to Begin On*. Holt, Rinehart and Winston, 1969.

Temko, Florence and Elaine Simon. *Paper Folding to Begin With*. Bobbs-Merrill Co. Inc., 1968.

✓Vermeer, Jackie and Marian Larivier. *The Little Kid's Craft Book*. Taplinger Publ. Co., 1973.

West, Robin. *Dinosaur Discoveries, How to Create Your Own Prehistoric World*. Carolrhoda Books Inc., 1989.

Wright, Lyndie. *Puppets*. Franklin Watts, 1989.

3. RECOMMENDED BOOKS FOR HIGH SCHOOL AND ADVANCED STUDENTS

The following list contains art books I have read and recommend for your child. This is not a complete list of art books available. You can order some of these books through local book store or art supply store, or you can ask your reference librarian to find them in the library or through the inter-library loan system.

Your child will need three kinds of art books: a reference explaining the elements and principles of design, a book on the history of the art medium he is studying, and a book explaining how to use this medium. He will be referring to these books quite often, so purchasing them for his personal library is a good idea.

One book that my fellow art teachers and I recommend highly that you purchase for your child is *Art Talk*, by Rosalind Ragans (Glencoe Publishing Co., P.O. Box 508, Columbus, OH 43272-4174). It is easy to read, well-written, full of information about the elements of art and the principles of design, and contains many beautiful photographs of famous artwork. It is written for junior high and high school students.

Architecture and Interior Design

Dunn, Alan. *Architecture Observed* (a cartoon book). Architecture Record Books, 1971.

Emmerling, Mary. *American Country West*. Clarkson Potter Publ. Inc., 1985.

Korab, Balthazar. *Archabet*. National Trust for Historic Preservation, 1985.

Kostof, Spiro. *History of Architecture, Setting and Rituals*. Oxford University Press, 1985.

Lewis, Roger K. *Architect, A Candid Guide to the Profession*. MIT Press, 1985.

Old and New, Architectural Design Relationship. Taken from a conference sponsored by The National Trust for Historic Preservation. The Preservation Press, 1980.

Yarwood, Doreen. *A Chronology of Western Architecture*. Facts on File Publications, 1987.

Art Appreciation and History

Cantacuzino, Sherban. *Re-Architecture: Old Buildings/New Uses.* Abbeville Press Publ., 1989.

Clar, Judson. *Design in America 1925-1950.* Harry N. Abrams Inc., 1983.

Ferrier, Jean-Louis. *Art of Our Century: The Chronicle of Western Art 1900 to the Present.* Prentice-Hall, 1988.

Freeman, Phyllis. *New Art.* Harry N. Abrams Inc., 1987.

Hunter, Sam and John Jacobus. *Modern Art: Painting, Sculpture, and Architecture.* Harry N. Abrams Inc., 1985.

Janson, H.W. and Anthony F. Janson. *History of Art for Young People.* Harry N. Abrams Inc., 1987.

Klotz, Heinrich. *Twentieth Century Architecture.* Rizzoli, 1989.

Lucie-Smith, Edward. *Late Modern, The Visual Arts Since 1945.* Frederick A. Praeger Publ., 1969.

Mathey, Francois. *The Impressionists.* Frederick A. Praeger, 1967.

McCoy, Garnett. *David Smith* (sculptures form 1930 to 1960). Frederick A. Praeger, 1973.

Moore, Janet Gaylord. *The Many Ways of Seeing, An Introduction to the Pleasures of Art.* The World Publ. Co., 1968.

Moszynska, Anna. *Abstract Art.* Thames and Hudson, 1990.

Read, Herbert. *A Concise History of Modern Sculpture.* Frederick A. Praeger, 1968.

Redstone, Louis. *Public Art, New Directions.* McGraw-Hill Book Co., 1981.

Tunnard, Christopher and Pushkarev, Boris. *Man-Made America.* Harmony Books, 1981 (a National Book Award winner).

Crafts

Babington, Audrey. *Creative Wall Hangings and Panels.* Arco Publ. Inc., 1982.

Boyles, Margaret. *Bargello: An Explosion in Color.* Macmillan Publ. Co. Inc., 1974.

Bullen, Jenny. *Starting Embroidery.* B.T. Batsford Ltd., 1989.

Cataldo, John W. *Lettering.* Davis Publ. Inc., 1974.

Davis, Mary Kay. *The Needlework Doctor: How to Solve Every Kind of Needlework Problem.* Prentice-Hall Inc., 1982.

Hall, Carolyn Vosburg. *Soft Sculpture.* Davis Publ. Inc., 1981.

Hawcock, David. *Art From Paper.* Crescent Books, 1987.

Highstone, John. *Wirecraft*. Houghton Mifflin, 1978.

Illustrated Library of Arts and Crafts 4 vols. Fuller and Dees, 1974.

Jarnow, Jill. *Sampler Stitchery*. Doubleday and Co., 1982.

Johnson, Mary Elizabeth. *Pillows, Designs, Patterns, Projects*. Oxmoor House Inc., 1978.

Kenny, John B. *Ceramic Design*. Chilton Book Co., 1971.

Litherland, Janet. *The Banner Handbook*. Meriwether Publ. Ltd., 1987.

Meilach, Dona Z. *Box Art*. Crown Publ. Inc., 1975.

_____. *Creating Art From Anything: Ideas, Materials, Techniques*. Galahad Books, 1968.

Needlework School. Chartwell Books Inc., 1984.

Nelson, Glenn C. *Ceramics*. Holt, Rinehart and Winston Inc., 1960.

Rhodes, Daniel. *Clay and Glazes for the Potter*. Chilton Book Co., 1973.

St. George, Amelia. *The Stencil Book*. E.P. Dutton, 1988.

Shaw, George Russell. *Knots, Useful and Ornamental, Fully Illustrated*. Collier Books, 1974.

Sprintzen, Alice. *Crafts, Contemporary Design and Techniques* (paper, fiber, clay, glass, leather, metal, scrimshaw). Davis Publ. Inc., 1987.

Vanderbilt, Gloria. *Book of Collage*. Van Nostrand Reinhold, 1970.

Walpole, Lois. *Creative Basket Making*. North Light Books, 1989.

Drawing

Adams, Norman and Joe Singer. *Drawing Animals*. Watson-Guptill, 1979.

Barry, Bill. *The World of Cartooning*. Bill Barry Enterprises, CB Publ., 1989.

Bridgman, George B. *The Book of a Hundred Hands*. Bridgman Publ., 1920.

Dodson, Bert. *Keys to Drawing*. North Light Books, 1985.

Downer, Marion. *Discovering Design*. Lothrop, Lee and Shepard Co., 1947.

Edwards, Betty. *Drawing on the Artist Within, An Inspirational and Practical Guide to Increasing Your Creative Powers*. Simon and Schuster, 1986.

Gerberg, Mort. *Cartooning*. Arbor House, 1983.

Gordon, Louise. *How to Draw the Human Head: Techniques and*

Anatomy. Penguin Books, 1977.

Gollwitzer, Gerard. *The Joy of Drawing*. Gramercy Publ. Co., 1959.

Jardine, Don L. *Creating Cartoon Characters*. Walter Foster, 1989.

Lent, William T. *Speed Sketching: A Modern Approach to the Art of Sketching for Beginners and Professionals Alike*. Doubleday and Co. Inc., 1978.

Lohan, Frank J. *Pen and Ink, Step by Step*. Contemporary Books Inc., 1983.

Sarnoff, Bob. *Cartoons and Comics*. Davis Publ., 1988.

Sloane, E. *Illustrating Fashion*. Harper and Row Publ., 1977.

Weiss, Harvey. *Cartoons and Cartooning*. Houghton Mifflin, 1990.

Painting

Browning, Colleen. *Working Out A Painting*. Watson-Guptill Publ., 1988.

Duckett, Graham. *Airbrush, A Step by Step Guide to Technical Skills and Equipment*. Collier Books, Macmillan Publ. Co., 1985.

Crawshaw, Alwyn. *How to Paint with Watercolors*. HP Books, 1986.

Garrard, Peter and John Garrard. *How to Paint with Oils*. HP Books, 1986.

Gorrwge, Roger and Ted Gould. *Airbrush Course*. Van Nostrand Reinhold, 1989.

Monahan, Patricia. *You Can Paint Portraits*. North Light Press, 1985.

Johnson, Peter D. *Painting With Pastels*. North Light Press, 1984.

Hill, Tom. *Color for the Watercolor Painter*. Watson-Guptill Publ., 1975.

Mayer, Ralph. *The Painter's Craft: An Introduction of Artists' Methods and Materials*. Penguin Books, 1982.

Mayer, Ralph. *The Artist's Handbook of Materials and Techniques*. Penguin Books, 1982.

Parramon, Jose M. and G. Fresquet. *How to Paint in Watercolor*. HP Books, 1982.

Roddon, Guy. *Pastel Painting Techniques*. North Light Press, 1987.

Tate, Elizabeth. *The North Light Illustrated Book of Painting Techniques*. North Light, Quanto Publishers, 1986.

Whitney, Edgar. *Complete Guide to Watercolor Painting*. Watson-Guptill Publ., 1974.

Sculpture

Beecroft, Glynis. *Carving Techniques.* Arco Publ. Inc., 1982.

Finn, David. *How to Look at Sculpture.* Harry N. Abrams Inc., 1989.

Hammacher, A.M. *Modern Sculpture, Tradition and Innovation* (enlarged edition). Harry N. Abrams Inc., 1988.

Naylor, Rod. *Woodcarving Techniques.* B.T. Batsford Ltd., 1979.

Verhelst, Wilbert. *Sculpture: Tools, Materials and Techniques.* Prentice-Hall Inc., 1973.

Miscellaneous

Abling, Bina. *Fashion Sketchbook.* Fairchild Publ., 1988.

Brommer, Gerald and Joseph A. Gatto. *Careers in Art, An Illustrated Guide.* Davis Publ. Co., 1984.

Conner, Susan. *Artist's Market.* Writer's Digest. Published annually.

Ito, Dee. *The School of Visual Arts Guide to Careers.* McGraw-Hill Book Co., 1987.

Roukes, Nicholas. *Art Synectics, Stimulating Creativity in Art.* Davis Publ. Inc., 1982.

Worton, Hayes. *Essentials of Photography.* Glencoe, Macmillan/McGraw-Hill, 1988.

4. MAGAZINES FOR YOUR CHILD

Children enjoy getting their own magazines. If you would like to order a magazine for your child, use the following information. Most publishers will send you a trial issue free or for the cost of postage.

Magazines for the Younger Artist

Art-Line, News and Views for Young Artists
RR #1, Box 367
Rockville, IN 47872

This is a new publication, founded by the author of this book, just for kids.

Cricket
Carus Publication Company
315 5th St.
Peru, IL 61354

Cricket is a magazine full of wonderful children's stories accompanied by drawings that will be enjoyed by young artists.

National Geographic World
National Geographic Society
Washington, DC 20036

Beautiful magazine full of photographs of animals that your child can use for help with drawing and sculpture. Inexpensive; published monthly.

Surprises
275 Market St., Suite 521
Minneapolis, MN 55405

Magazine full of activities for children. Moderately priced; published bimonthly.

Your Big Backyard and *Ranger Rick*
National Wildlife Federation
8925 Leesburg Pike
Vienna, VA 22075

Two beautiful magazines with lots of photographs. Inexpensive; published monthly.

Zoobooks
Wildlife Education Ltd.
3590 Kettner Blvd.
San Diego, CA 92101

Beautiful magazine with good photos of animals. Inexpensive; published monthly.

Magazines for the Young Adult

American Artist
1 Color Ct.
Marion, OH 43305

Beautiful magazine with both contemporary and traditional art styles. Has how-to articles as well as success stories. Very informative and beautifully photographed. Moderately priced; published monthly.

American Craft
American Craft Council
72 Spring St.
New York, NY 10012

Contemporary crafts only. Expensive; published bimonthly.

Art in America
Brant Art Publications Inc.
575 Broadway
New York, NY 10012

Beautiful magazine about American art in the past and present. Expensive; published monthly.

Art Students League News
Art Students League of New York
215 W. 57th St.
New York, NY 10019

Creative Ideas for Living
707 Kautz Rd.
St. Charles, IL 60174

Interesting magazine full of creative ideas for making daily life more beautiful, interesting, and efficient. Moderately priced; published bimonthly.

Designing Eye
Tartan Group
1255 Woodland Ave.
Batavia, IL 60510-3051

For interior designers. Moderately priced; published monthly.

Graphic Studio News
Graphic New York CMC Publishers
210 E. 38th St. #3E
New York, NY 10016

Moderately priced; published monthly.

National Geographic
P.O. Box 2895
Washington, DC 20077-9960

Highly recommended for its beautiful and interesting photographs. Moderately priced; published monthly.

Popular Photography
Diamond Communications, Inc.
1515 Broadway
New York, NY 10036

Moderately priced; published monthly.

BIBLIOGRAPHY

Dubman, Sheila, Ellen Andrews, and Mary Lewis Hansen. *Exploring Visual Arts and Crafts Careers*. Washington: U.S. Government Printing Office, 1976.

Edwards, Betty. *Drawing on the Artist Within*. New York: Simon and Schuster, 1986.

Feldman, Dr. Beverly N. *Kids Who Succeed*. New York: Rawson Associates, 1987.

Ginott, Dr. Haim G. *Between Parent and Child*. New York: Avon Books, 1956.

Haubenstock, Susan H. and David Joselit. *Career Opportunities in Art*. New York: Facts on File Publications, 1988.

Hawes, Carolyn, Margaret Johnson, and Judith Nylen. *Your Career in Art and Design*. New York: Arco Publ. Co. Inc., 1978.

Holden, Donald. *Art Career Guide*. New York: Watson-Guptill Publ., 1983.

Jevnikar, Jana. *Careers in the Arts: A Resource Guide*. New York: Center for Arts Information—Opportunity Resources for the Arts, 1981.

Leistico, Agnes. *I Learn Better By Teaching Myself*. Tonasket, WA: Home Education Press, 1990.

Mitchell, Dr. William and Dr. Charles Paul Conn. *The Power of Positive Parenting*. New York: Wynwood Press, 1989.

Peale, Norman Vincent. *The Power of Positive Thinking*. Prentice-Hall Inc., 1952.

Plaskow, Daphne. *Art With Children*. New York: Watson-Guptill Publ., 1968.

Ragans, Rosalind. *Art Talk*. Mission Hills, CA: Glencoe Publ. Co., 1988.

Silberstein-Storfer, Muriel. *Doing Art Together*. New York: Simon and Schuster, 1982.

Tripp, Rhonda Thomas. *The International Thesaurus of Quotations*. New York: Thomas Y. Crowell Publishers, 1970.

Wachowiak, Frank and Theodore Ramsay. *Emphasis Art*. Scranton, PA: International Textbook Co., 1965.

INDEX